T0270408

UNSTUCK

90 Days of Inspiration, Encouragement, and the Promise of New Life

REAL TALK KIM

EMANATE
BOOKS

Published in Nashville, Tennessee, by Emanate Books, an imprint of Thomas Nelson. Emanate Books and Thomas Nelson are registered trademarks of HarperCollins Christian Publishing, Inc.

Author is represented by the literary agency of The FEDD Agency, Inc., Post Office Box 341973, Austin, Texas 78734.

Thomas Nelson titles may be purchased in bulk for educational, business, fundraising, or sales promotional use. For information, please email SpecialMarkets@ThomasNelson.com.

Library of Congress Cataloging-in-Publication Data

Names: Real Talk Kim, author.
Title: Unstuck : 90 days of inspiration, encouragement, and the promise of new life / Real Talk Kim.
Description: Nashville, Tennessee : Emanate, [2024] | Summary: "Real Talk Kim offers ninety days of encouragement and motivation to help readers conquer their everyday struggles and follow God's plan for them to get unstuck from regrets, shame, and broken dreams"-- Provided by publisher.
Identifiers: LCCN 2024005587 (print) | LCCN 2024005588 (ebook) | ISBN 9781400242153 (hardcover) | ISBN 9781400242177 (ebook)
Subjects: LCSH: Thought and thinking--Religious aspects--Christianity. | Resilience (Personality trait) | Self-actualization (Psychology)--Religious aspects--Christianity.
Classification: LCC BV4598.4 .R4258 2024 (print) | LCC BV4598.4 (ebook) | DDC 248.4--dc23 /eng/20240429
LC record available at https://lccn.loc.gov/2024005587
LC ebook record available at https://lccn.loc.gov/2024005588

Printed in the United States of America

24 25 26 27 28 LBC 5 4 3 2 1

Day 1

ANTICIPATE YOUR NEXT

Then Joshua told the people, "Purify yourselves, for tomorrow the LORD will do great wonders among you."
—JOSHUA 3:5

For forty years, the children of Israel had wandered in the wilderness. They were saved from the slavery of Egypt but, because of their unbelief, they lived a defeated life when they should have been entering their rest in the promised land. A whole generation had died and was buried in the wilderness, and the next generation was waiting to enter the new land. After Moses died, God chose Joshua as the next leader. Joshua was about to lead the Israelites across the Jordan River. He knew if the Israelites did not follow him unquestioningly, they would fail in their mission. They should have easily understood the importance of the task at hand as they had watched countless thousands die because of disobedience while journeying through the wilderness.

Remember: God called Israel out of Egypt and redeemed them from slavery. They were to keep their focus on Him and remain separate from the Gentiles. Joshua gave them the direct command: "Purify yourselves, for tomorrow the LORD will do great wonders among you." He was telling them to anticipate their next steps. The following day, God did what He had promised. He stopped the fast-flowing waters of the Jordan, and the people crossed over safely.

Just as God promised to do wonders among the children of Israel, we also have His promises of wonders in our lifetime. I wonder how many opportunities we miss because we fear the unknown instead of *anticipating our next*. We have been told that the eye has not seen and the ear has not heard the wonderful things that God has prepared for those who love Him (1 Corinthians 2:9). Caleb, one of the twelve spies along with Joshua, was promised his own mountain in the promised land, and he claimed that mountain when he was eighty-five years old. He remembered what God had told him forty-five years earlier, and he held on to that promise.

———————

Father, give me the insight to walk by faith and not by sight. I will claim Your promises over my life. In Jesus' name, amen.

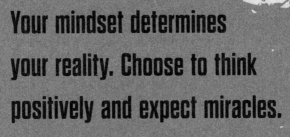

Your mindset determines your reality. Choose to think positively and expect miracles.

—RTK

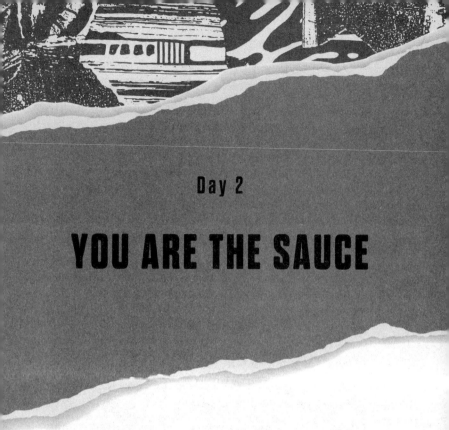

Day 2

YOU ARE THE SAUCE

As Samuel grew up, the LORD was with him, and everything Samuel said proved to be reliable.

—1 SAMUEL 3:19

Samuel is a Bible character who models for me a close relationship with Jesus Christ. Samuel was born as a result of his barren mother's prayer. Hannah, Samuel's mother, promised she would give her baby back to God if

He would just bless her with a son. She followed through on her promise and when Samuel was a young boy he was taken to the tabernacle to live with Eli, who was a high priest and a judge. Samuel began to grow in the knowledge of God, and his world revolved around serving at the tabernacle.

Three separate times one night Samuel thought he heard Eli calling him. Finally, Eli realized it was God and told Samuel to answer God: "Speak, your servant is listening" (1 Samuel 3:10). Samuel began forming a relationship with God. He learned to listen to God's voice and learned that God speaks to those who listen. Samuel was developing his own sauce. Our scripture says that Samuel grew, the Lord was with him, and everything Samuel said proved to be reliable. He never took God's love for granted but nourished it even after years of serving God. Samuel's sauce was the consistent obedience of doing the will of the Father.

God enjoys conversations with His children, and He is waiting for you to spend time in His presence. I remember the constant fear of failure as a child carrying the label "learning disabled." No matter how much my mother studied with me and rehearsed words and stories, I was unable to remember what I had so diligently studied the previous evening. My teachers constantly focused on my inconsistencies and inabilities; however, I determined I would make a difference. I realized I had the ability to lead and make people laugh. I could hold everyone's attention even though I may not have remembered my report. I could easily cover up my struggles.

As I developed a true relationship with Jesus Christ at forty years old, I began spending countless hours in God's Word. I determined I would be the speaker God had called me to be. People are amazed today as I quote hundreds of verses by memory and retell well-loved Bible stories. I developed my own sauce as Samuel had done. I could not become a Samuel, but I could become the girl God had anointed and appointed me to be, the girl to make a difference. He has a distinct call for you. It's time for you to get unstuck, rise up, soar, and make a difference.

Father, as I find my place in the body of Christ, shine Your light on my path. May I develop into the instrument of worship that You have called me to be. In Jesus' name, amen.

Day 3

BEAUTIFULLY BROKEN

> To all who mourn in Israel,
> he will give a crown of beauty for ashes,
> a joyous blessing instead of mourning,
> festive praise instead of despair.
> —Isaiah 61:3

As I reread this uplifting passage, my mind goes back to the season when I was so broken that I thought I would never see any semblance of normal again. I had two sons, nine and eleven, who looked to me to make their world normal, but I was unable to move past the broken marriage or the loss of my business and home to see a new tomorrow.

I now know that we, too, must do our part to see change in our lives. Change doesn't happen just because we want it. It happens because we make up our minds to do something different.

It becomes easier and easier to fail when you fall enough times. I love the psalmist David because he fell time and time again, yet he called out to God for mercy in his most troubling times. I, too, learned to call out to God for mercy as I was drowning in despair. When I wrote the book *Beautifully Broken*, I had two sons depending on me. Do you have certain ones today counting on you to make a change?

If I can make it, so can you.

Father, I cry out for mercy and fall into Your arms as I face this day and determine I will make changes. In Jesus' name, amen.

COUNT YOUR BLESSINGS

Let all that I am praise the LORD;
may I never forget the good things he
does for me.
—PSALM 103:2

David, the writer of this psalm, knew the importance of counting his blessings. He was one of eight sons of Jesse, out of whose family the next king would come. When God told the prophet Samuel that He would choose one of Jesse's sons to be anointed king, the family never considered the shepherd boy David as a possibility. David wasn't even called in from the fields as the prophet scoped out his brothers.

After Samuel realized the future king was not standing in his presence, he asked if there was another son. David was then called in and anointed as the future king. David, the least of eight sons, was not only chosen by God to be the next king but God also said that David was a man after His own heart (1 Samuel 13:14).

I can so relate to David as I stand before thousands weekly, giving away the love that God has given to me. I was the "least" of my family. My brother was the model child who at the age of twenty-three stepped into a senior pastor position at my parents' church. I was the black sheep of the family who did not get it together until I was thirty-eight years old, when I began a journey of renewal while seeking the Father's will for my life. I'm thankful for my blessings as I excitedly open my eyes each morning to a brand-new day of service in the kingdom of God.

Father, give me the opportunity to praise Your name today as I remember the blessings I have been given—including breath, health, family, and a job. Help me respond to others with the love You have given to me. In Jesus' name, amen.

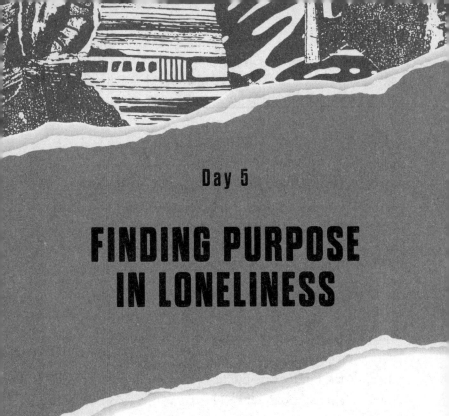

Day 5

FINDING PURPOSE IN LONELINESS

Don't be afraid, for I am with you.
  Don't be discouraged, for I am your God.
I will strengthen you and help you.
  I will hold you up with my victorious
    right hand.

—ISAIAH 41:10

Bible promises keep us grounded despite our troubles. When God said not to be afraid, He knew we would face situations that made us tremble with fear, yet we could stand strong. Many of the psalms were written as David found himself hiding from enemies who were intent on killing him. If anyone knew times of loneliness, it would be this young man who had grown up on the hills of Israel while herding his father's sheep. When Samuel went to David's father's house to anoint the future king of Israel, David was the missing link. The prophet could not anoint the future king until David was summoned, because God had called David to be king.

But David was alone doing what he did every day, taking care of the sheep. David was becoming a strong warrior as he wrestled the lion who was trying to kill the sheep on the hillside. He became accustomed to relying on God's strength while alone doing his father's business. When in the caves hiding from his enemies, he did not allow loneliness to rob him of his strength. He knew there was a purpose for being in the darkness. You, too, have purpose. You, too, face challenges. But when you understand there is a call for greater, you can rise up out of the darkness and take back all that has been stolen from you.

When you were born, doctors heard, "Waaah," but hell heard purpose, destiny, game-changer, nation-shifter, a person who can take a licking and keep on ticking. When God called you, He did not make a conference call. He called you and only you for your selected purpose. Remember that so you may find your purpose in times of loneliness.

Father, show me my purpose and give me a plan of action to get unstuck and take back all that has been stolen from me. In Jesus' name, amen.

Day 6

NOTHING IS IMPOSSIBLE

David said, "What have I done now? Is there not a cause?"

—1 SAMUEL 17:29 NKJV

T he biblical account of David and Goliath is one of the most popular stories in the Bible. This young shepherd boy, who had stayed home while his brothers were fighting in Saul's army, was sent by his father to visit the front lines and bring back news of the battle. As he arrived he heard the Philistines ridiculing the Israelite forces, who were trembling with fear as the giant Goliath mocked not only Israel but also their God. David's brother Eliab saw him and asked, "Why did you come?" David's answer—"Is there not a cause?"—was an indictment of his brother's fear and lack of faith. The fearful Israelites wanted freedom but were unwilling to go after the giant who was taunting them.

After David persuaded Saul to let him defend Israel's honor, he carried his sling and five small stones to face their dreaded enemy in what appeared to be an impossible situation. David put a rock in his sling and swung it. The rock sank into the giant's forehead, and he fell. David picked up Goliath's sword and used it to cut off his head. The Philistines turned and ran when they saw a shepherd boy had struck down their hero. Israel won the battle because David trusted God.

Each of us has our own kind of giants. I wonder what giants you are facing today. David's greatest battles in his early years were not against the lion or the bear he slew while protecting his father's sheep. His greatest obstacles were created by those close to him who tried to put limitations on him.

Even his own father did not see his potential. When the prophet Samuel came to anoint the future king, Jesse called all his sons except David to stand before Samuel. Yet God knew He had anointed and appointed David, the less-than, the unknown, the youngest, to be the next king. As you walk into your new day, remember David and the obstacles that could not defeat him. You were chosen to be you. God has a plan and that is to do you good. Nothing can stop you when you understand your purpose—nothing is impossible with God.

Father, give me the understanding to move when You speak. Help me stay in Your Word so I can have the mind of Christ. In Jesus' name, amen.

Day 7

BOUNCE BACK

God removed Saul and replaced him with David, a man about whom God said, "I have found David son of Jesse, a man after my own heart. He will do everything I want him to do."

—Acts 13:22

Most people take the phrase "man after my own heart" as a reference to David's moral character. David was a man after God's own heart in that he was committed to God's ways and demonstrated allegiance to God's law. On one hand, however, David was far from morally pure. He was a murderous adulterer. On the other hand, David showed himself to be the opposite of Saul, his predecessor, in every way. He waited upon the Lord and sought God's will above his own. Even in his sin David was sensitive to obey when the prophet Nathan called him out.

What was it that made David so different that God referred to him as a man after His own heart? When Absalom—David's son who would have killed him if he'd had the chance—was killed by David's mighty men, David wished he could have died in his son's place. That is the heart of God, willing to die for us while knowing that we do not deserve mercy but desperate to give it to us anyway. He gives us the chance to get up one more time and bounce back. David could not die for his son, but God could die for His children, and He did.

Father, as I face my failures, give me the strength to get up again and face tomorrow while knowing that You are with me. In Jesus' name, amen.

Day 8

MOVE ON

*No, dear brothers and sisters, I have not
achieved it, but I focus on this one thing:
Forgetting the past and looking forward to what
lies ahead, I press on to reach the end of the
race and receive the heavenly prize for which
God, through Christ Jesus, is calling us.*
—PHILIPPIANS 3:13–14

David was about fifteen years old when Samuel called
him in from the field to anoint him as king. It's not

clear how much time passed between his anointing and the slaying of Goliath. David then, after slaying Goliath, waited fifteen years to become king; however, he never got stuck.

Even though David's brothers were more likely to be chosen and had more experience than David, God had a different plan. When Jesse lined up his sons, the older and more advanced brothers were not chosen. Samuel even thought, *Surely one of these handsome young men will be the future king.*

Our tendency is to believe that God chooses the most talented, the one with the most charisma. However, God often chooses the most insignificant one to become the greatest in His kingdom. David was able not only to rule God's people as king, but as we've noted, David was a man after God's heart. David made many errors in judgment. He faltered and failed, but he repented and always came back to God.

In the New Testament we meet the apostle Paul, who considered himself the chief of sinners even though he was one of the most learned men in the Sanhedrin. Because Paul came face-to-face with the mercy and grace of Jesus, he was able to become an evangelist for the cause of Christ and wrote more than half of the New Testament. Just before Paul's conversion—when his name was still Saul—he was uttering threats and trying to kill as many Christians as possible. Then he had a personal encounter with the man called Jesus.

Paul moved from torturing the Christians of the early church to planting churches throughout Asia.

When we can be honest with ourselves, our old way of life will not rule us any longer. We will have a new way of thinking and be able to move from being a prisoner of sin to living a life of freedom. Follow David's and Paul's examples and get up, get unstuck, and make up your mind that this day will be unlike any day you have experienced. You can soar!

***

Father, today I focus on forgetting the past and looking ahead to my new life. In Jesus' name, amen.

Day 9

NEVER ALONE

You keep track of all my sorrows.
 You have collected all my tears
  in your bottle.
 You have recorded each one
  in your book.
My enemies will retreat when I call
 to you for help.
 This I know: God is on my side!
—Psalm 56:8–9

Psalm 56 was written when David was fleeing from King Saul, whose only interest at that time was David's death. David fled to Gath and pretended to be mentally unhinged for his own safety. What drove this fearless warrior to this state of mind instead of confidently knowing that God would take care of him?

David was driven by fear. He was exhausted and knew that if King Saul found him, he would be killed immediately. Fear cancels out faith. Fear can lead to wrongful actions and decisions.

David believed that God was with him despite his wrong decisions. He knew that God's hand remained upon him, and it was as though God was catching every tear that fell down his cheek. This psalm brought me great solace during my time of failure and loss when I felt that no one understood me or my circumstances. If David, who would become an adulterer and a murderer, could still have that personal relationship with God in a time of need, I knew I wanted to understand this God who would accept me as His daughter even though I had failed miserably.

I thank God daily for my time of failure because it was during this time that I found my Rock, Jesus Christ. I had never had a true personal relationship with Him. I did not feel worthy of His forgiveness, yet He extended the same grace to me that David experienced. Even in my failure, I was not alone. I know now that Jesus never left me nor forsook me.

Father, as I humbly come to You, I give You thanks for allowing me to hit rock bottom and find the Rock. I know You love me despite my failures. Thank You for never leaving me alone. In Jesus' name, amen.

Day 10

PEACE OVER PIECES

Don't worry about anything; instead, pray about everything. Tell God what you need, and thank him for all he has done. Then you will experience God's peace, which exceeds anything we can understand. His peace will guard your hearts and minds as you live in Christ Jesus.

—Philippians 4:6–7

26

Under house arrest as a prisoner of the Roman government, Paul sent a letter of thanksgiving to the church in Philippi. He was chained to a soldier in an apartment in Rome, unsure of his future, yet he made sure the church that he started in Philippi was encouraged to find that although he was a prisoner, he was still free in his spirit. Paul was in prison, for sure, but the gospel was not. Even as a prisoner, Paul wrote about praying, avoiding worry, and finding the joy and peace of the Lord. He wrote about the blessings that had come to him from Christians who had supported him in his time of need.

Paul described how Jesus lowered Himself to serve others, and he urged Jesus' disciples to have the same mindset. Paul had no idea if he would ever be released or if his end would be in this Roman imprisonment; however, he challenged the Philippian converts to imitate his example by giving up everything for Christ. He told them that whether he was sufficiently blessed or in poverty, he had become content in whatever state he was in. Paul chose peace over pieces. The summary of Paul's life was extraordinary: "For to me, to live is Christ and to die is gain" (Philippians 1:21 NIV). Paul understood that the meaning of life is to serve Christ at all costs.

Father, give me the understanding of how to live a life filled with peace. Help me give my frustrations to You and accept the peace that will guard my heart and mind. In Jesus' name, amen.

FOCUS

Fix your thoughts on what is true, and honorable, and right, and pure, and lovely, and admirable. Think about things that are excellent and worthy of praise.

—PHILIPPIANS 4:8

If someone were keeping a record of your thoughts, would you allow them to be publicly displayed? Would you be so focused on the negatives that you have no room for the positives, or would you be the one who always sees life through rose-colored glasses?

When writing to the Philippians, the apostle Paul was a prisoner because he was a believer in Jesus Christ and would not recant the gospel. He encouraged the Christians in Philippi not only to seek God but also to believe that no matter the circumstances, they would receive a peace that would sustain them in the most troubling times when they gave their all to Jesus Christ.

It's easy to dwell on the negatives when life is hard, disappointing, or painful. When the enemy tries to destroy you, he puts lies and condemnation in your mind. If he can get you to believe that your life, as it is, offers you no hope, he will win the battle for your mind, which is the greatest battle you will face.

Christians are not to allow despair, sadness, anger, or bitterness to control our reactions. To dwell on those things that are good and pure and holy is radically different from the ways of this broken world. Yet the answer to winning the battle for our minds is to reclaim and live out our lives with love, hope, faith, and forgiveness, which bring us peace.

Focus on those things that are good and allow Jesus to fill you with His peace that surpasses all understanding.

Father, give me the strength and wisdom to face my tomorrows with the peace that comes from serving You. In Jesus' name, amen.

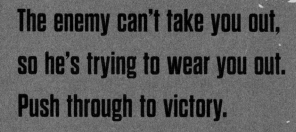

The enemy can't take you out,
so he's trying to wear you out.
Push through to victory.

—RTK

BELIEVE IN YOU

For I can do everything through Christ,
who gives me strength.

—Philippians 4:13

Paul is one of my favorite Bible heroes. This man, who had an extensive education in the Jewish faith, forsook all to follow Jesus Christ. Paul was on his way to persecute and possibly even kill Christians when he had a personal visitation from Jesus on the road to Damascus. The result? His life was changed and he wrote more than half the books of the New Testament. He wrote today's scripture to the Philippian church while he was locked up in prison because he would not forsake his belief in the power of Jesus Christ. No matter his circumstances, he did not flinch when encountering persecution.

Paul's example of standing despite the circumstances gives me encouragement as I daily minister to thousands on various social media platforms. Knowing how Paul faced his accusers and stood firm in the middle of the trials gives me faith that I, too, can stand. Quote Philippians 4:13 throughout today and allow it to become your reality.

When you believe this verse, nothing can steal your purpose. Remember, God did not take time to make a nobody. He made everybody special. You are special!

Father, my heart is full of thanksgiving for all the blessings given me despite my failures. I know when You chose me that You knew I would fail in many situations, and You still trusted me to get up one more time than I fall down. Allow me to stand in trying times through Your strength. In Jesus' name, amen.

Day 13

LOVE LIFE

*Love is patient and kind. Love is not jealous or
boastful or proud or rude. It does not demand
its own way. It is not irritable, and it keeps
no record of being wronged. It does not rejoice
about injustice but rejoices whenever the truth
wins out. Love never gives up, never loses faith,
is always hopeful, and endures through every
circumstance.*

—1 CORINTHIANS 13:4–7

The apostle Paul often gave testimony about how his love for Jesus Christ changed his life. When he received Jesus as Lord of his life, he began the journey of love that we study today. The love that Paul received led him through years of service to others. He had no problem laying down his life daily for the gospel of Jesus Christ.

We each must make decisions that will propel us into our next season. We can easily remain stagnant and allow life to steal our dreams, or we can arise daily, knowing that we will make a difference in someone's life by representing Jesus' unyielding love.

My daily prayer is that I never again allow life to steal my focus from doing the will of the Father. Because we share life with those who do not understand the importance of love, it is up to us to always respond as Jesus would. In those times of distrust and misunderstanding, we can show those who share life with us that we have found a reason for blessing even when blessings are not deserved.

Today, make the decision to see good in others even when good is hard to find. Determine that you will be the difference in making their day or setting things straight. We don't always have to be right, but we must always love.

Father, as I face this day, help me bless and not curse. Let me see the good in others and let them see Jesus in me. In Jesus' name, amen.

Day 14

QUIT QUITTING

The Spirit of God, who raised Jesus from the dead, lives in you. And just as God raised Christ Jesus from the dead, he will give life to your mortal bodies by this same Spirit living within you.

—ROMANS 8:11

The Bible doesn't teach quitting. Even though God has called us to an abundant life, we all go through seasons of challenges. Paul wrote that the same Spirit that raised Jesus from the dead lives in us. Paul understood the strength of being filled with the Spirit. Even though he went through numerous trials, he did not quit or become defeated.

Paul, falsely accused and imprisoned, was transported by ship to Rome under military escort. Heavy storms blew the ship off course and caused it to break up near the island of Malta. One person on board, however, had hope, and that person was Paul. An angel visited Paul, who was able to give everyone on board the word that they would make it safely to shore. The ship's crew realized that Paul's spiritual insight was important for their survival.

While building a fire on the beach after their safe landing, Paul was bitten by a snake but survived. The islanders thought Paul was a god. *Who is bitten by a venomous snake and lives?* they thought. Then Publius, the chief official of the island, asked Paul to pray for his sick father. After Publius's father was healed, others began coming for prayer. Life was going well for Paul.

Three months later, the group boarded another ship headed for Rome and Paul was on his way to prison. His life was one challenge after another.

God knows what He's doing. He makes no mistakes. We are not governed by bad luck or good luck, but we are covered by the blood of Jesus Christ. Problems and difficulties do not stop God from working His plan. Not even a fierce storm and a snake bite could keep Paul from his destination. Problems, difficulties, sicknesses, and dangers will come, but we have the assurance that God will work all things together for our good (Romans 8:28).

━━━━━━━━━

Father, as I walk out Your plan for my life, give me the faith to believe that You are working all things together for my good. In Jesus' name, amen.

Day 15

RENEW YOUR MIND

Don't copy the behavior and customs of this world, but let God transform you into a new person by changing the way you think. Then you will learn to know God's will for you, which is good and pleasing and perfect.

—ROMANS 12:2

Renewing your mind is a transforming journey at the heart of your spiritual growth. In a fast-paced world filled with countless distractions and conflicting influences, it's easy to absorb worldly values and lose sight of your divine purpose. Paul calls us to a higher standard through Christ Jesus, to be nonconformists to the pattern of this world and to allow God to reshape our thinking. This can only happen as we get in His Word and allow it to penetrate our thoughts and actions.

Renewing our minds is not just a mental exercise that we practice daily as we do our physical exercises. It is a commitment to immerse ourselves in Scripture and prayer. As we allow God's Word to wash over us daily, our thoughts align with His. We see through His eyes, hear through His ears, and speak the words that He gives us to say. We become examples of Jesus Christ living and breathing in this society. We shed old mindsets that no longer serve us and embrace transformed lives that look like Christ's.

Through daily meditation on the Word and intentional prayer, we create a sacred space for Jesus to work in and through us. We do not rely on yesterday's experiences but reach into His presence daily to receive newness of life.

Father, today I invite You to move in and through me as I experience Your presence. I want Your anointing to transform my being from the inside out. In Jesus' name, amen.

Day 16

BETTER DAYS AHEAD

Yet I am confident I will see the LORD's goodness while I am here in the land of the living.

—PSALM 27:13

The story of Job in the Bible is about a confident man who had a heart for God. God testified that there was no man like Job on earth. He was described as a good man with a wife and ten children as well as many herds of animals and great wealth.

Then the Lord allowed Job's faith to be tested, and he faced loss of children, wealth, and even his physical health. Job's story reminds us that there is a spiritual conflict going on behind the scenes in our lives.

When my dad was diagnosed with dementia, we never dreamed that he would eventually pass from complications of the dreaded disease. During a five-year journey we watched the man who was a leader, mentor, pastor, spiritual father, and the greatest dad anyone could imagine begin to lose his memory a little more each day. My mom, brother, and I stood on the Word of God that he was covered by the blood of Jesus and no weapon formed against him would prosper.

My prayer partners around the world were praying my dad would come back to us. And as he made his final journey to his forever home, we were praising Jesus for the legacy he was leaving behind. I am now pastoring his church, Limitless. My mom has become a writer and an author. My brother faithfully leads our family. My sons, my dad's grandsons, have matured in the Lord.

In your darkness, it can be hard to believe that better days are coming. Stand on your faith and watch God do His best for you.

Father, as I face different seasons and challenges, help me understand that You have my very best interests at heart. In Jesus' name, amen.

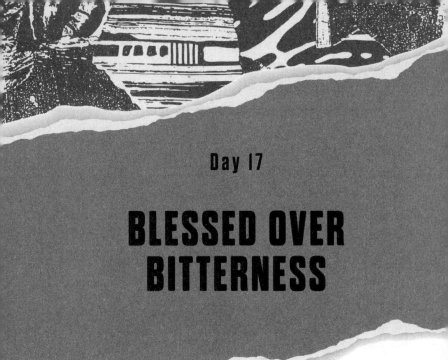

Day 17

BLESSED OVER BITTERNESS

"Don't call me Naomi," she responded. "Instead, call me Mara, for the Almighty has made life very bitter for me. I went away full, but the LORD has brought me home empty. Why call me Naomi when the LORD has caused me to suffer and the Almighty has sent such tragedy upon me?"

—RUTH 1:20–21

When Naomi and her husband, Elimelech, left Bethlehem they were looking for a new life without all the pain and lack they had been suffering. They had two sons who they believed deserved more than they were able to give them, so they headed for Moab. While this was a decision made out of a desire to survive, Moab was not the best place for Elimelech to take his family. He was leaving the promised land that God had given them and moving to Moab where the residents did not worship the Lord.

Elimelech died in Moab, leaving Naomi alone with her two sons. The sons married Moabite women, which was something God had wanted them to avoid. Ten years later, the sons died, leaving a household with three widows. Naomi heard that the famine had ended in Bethlehem and decided to go home. She urged her daughters-in-law to remain in Moab; however, Ruth refused and proclaimed that Naomi's God would be her God.

When she arrived in Bethlehem, Naomi told her family and friends to no longer call her Naomi but Mara, for the Almighty had dealt bitterly with her. She had lost the men in her life and now had the responsibility of caring for Ruth. But history shows how God can take bitterness and turn it into joy. Ruth met Boaz and eventually became his wife. Her son with Boaz was Obed, the father of Jesse and the grandfather of David. This woman from a heathen nation had a child who is in the lineage of Jesus

Christ. Naomi could never have orchestrated her life to bring about such honor and happiness.

———

Father, thank You that You have a plan and purpose for my life. I will walk in the steps You have orchestrated for me. In Jesus' name, amen.

DON'T JUST EXIST—LIVE

For in him we live and move and exist. As some of your own poets have said, "We are his offspring."

—Acts 17:28

From the moment we are born, we have an insatiable appetite for more. As children, we resent the restrictions, the boundaries of not being able to do whatever we desire. We try to grasp every experience, and some even go to the limits because they're never satisfied with the norm. Breaking norms can result in formal punishment such as fines or imprisonment or being rejected by those who do not understand.

We were created with the hunger to grow and grasp more and more because we were created by God in His image. He spoke the world into existence and separated water from land and light from darkness. Because He is the Creator of everything, we also are creative and strive to live and enjoy life without limits.

If we were created by God, then why the disconnect? Why do we often live such unfulfilling lives? Even though we were created by God and live and move through Him, we can only enjoy what He has given us when we have a true relationship with Him. Everything that God has made is for our enjoyment, but creation's ultimate purpose is to point us toward Him.

Live life to the fullest so that when you die, your gravestone won't be the only proof that you lived. To truly live means you must break free from the control of external things that rule your life. To be a victim to outside circumstances is to exist, but to be influenced by the internal is to live. Only Jesus Christ got life right. Nobody else even came close. We all want a blessed life, but a blessed life doesn't just happen. It's taking what God puts in front of us and working with it. My daily prayer is that I pursue the purpose He has already laid out for me and that I do it well.

Don't just exist—live.

Father, in everything I do and say, let me be connected to
Your purpose in spirit and truth. In Jesus' name, amen.

Day 19

FORGIVE YOURSELF

Peter said, "Man, I don't know what you are talking about." And immediately, while he was still speaking, the rooster crowed.

At that moment the Lord turned and looked at Peter. Suddenly, the Lord's words flashed through Peter's mind: "Before the rooster crows tomorrow morning, you will deny three times that you even know me."

—LUKE 22:60–61

As a prominent early church figure and part of Jesus' inner circle, Peter is featured in many of the stories in the four Gospels. There's a lot of emphasis on his reckless behavior, but the fact that he was a strong leader among the disciples could be the reason his behavior is emphasized. During the last Passover meal, Jesus mentioned that one of the disciples would betray him. This triggered an argument among the twelve over who was the best among them (Luke 22:24).

Jesus then turned His attention to Peter. Jesus alerted Peter that he would face a trial and that He was praying for him. After hearing Jesus' warning, Peter insisted that he was ready to die for the sake of the gospel. Jesus responded that, in fact, Peter would deny Him three times before the rooster crowed.

We know Peter did deny Jesus as He was escorted through the courtyard. Peter was shaken to remembrance on the third denial when the rooster crowed and Jesus looked straight at him. The heartbreak of realizing that he had fulfilled Jesus' prophecy was compounded by Jesus' presence.

Finally, Jesus addressed the issue. He told Peter that he would suffer for following Him, and then He issued the invitation He had delivered earlier: "Follow Me" (John 21:18–19). As Jesus did with Peter, He wants to heal us, restore us, and then invite us to recommit to follow Him even after we deny Him. Failure isn't fatal. Peter was given another chance to follow Christ. He is our example.

Father, each time I fail to respond to You, give me the courage to get up one more time than I fall down. In Jesus' name, amen.

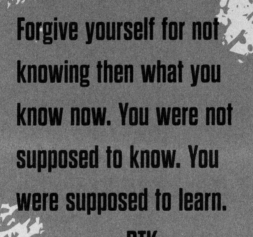

Forgive yourself for not knowing then what you know now. You were not supposed to know. You were supposed to learn.

—RTK

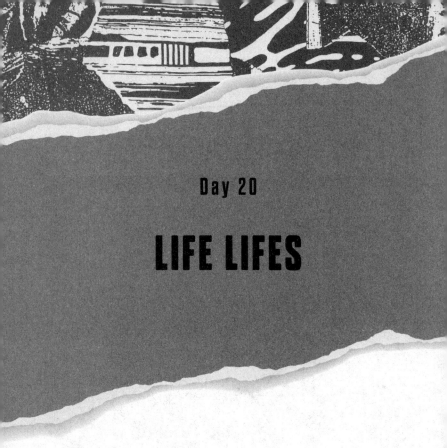

Day 20

LIFE LIFES

Yet God has made everything beautiful for its own time. He has planted eternity in the human heart, but even so, people cannot see the whole scope of God's work from beginning to end.

—ECCLESIASTES 3:11

We all go through many changes in life. Growing from children to adults, starting new jobs, or losing loved ones, we discover as we go through seasons of transition that life seldom remains the same.

Seasons of transition and change can be confusing, perplexing, and just plain scary. Several years ago a close friend was diagnosed with cancer. This vibrant young woman had always been excited about her tomorrows, and then everything changed. After a series of cancer treatments, she was told that she would not recover. One day, I went by to visit as her sisters were taking care of her needs. They had today's scripture playing softly as she rested. Even today when I think of her, I hear, "God has made everything beautiful for its own time."

The possibilities of what was ahead could have caused my friend to fear. But rather than be consumed by fear, my friend knew she was ready for her forever home, and she spoke life to everyone who came to visit.

My friend realized her days were shortened, yet she still praised Jesus and made peace with her Maker. Her example impacted my life even after my friend went to her forever home.

When we remember that we serve a God who knows the beginning and the end, it changes our perception of life's challenges. It's comforting to know that God is always with us as we face whatever life brings. We don't have to face it alone, and He already knows the future. My life quote is "life lifes." Even when we don't know what tomorrow holds, God holds all our tomorrows.

Father, we have not been guaranteed a certain number of days, and yet we know You are holding our todays and tomorrows in Your hand. Give us peace despite our challenges. In Jesus' name, amen.

LOVE, LOVE

Prophecy and speaking in unknown
languages and special knowledge will
become useless. But love will last forever!
—1 CORINTHIANS 13:8

The Bible is a book about love—romantic love, affectionate love, enduring love, playful love, unconditional love, and familiar love. I never really understood the power of love until I was in my darkest moment. It is true: sometimes you must hit rock bottom to be introduced to the Rock—Jesus Christ. We sometimes think love started at the cross when Jesus gave up for us His dignity, His life, His mother, and His friends. Then we see Jesus becoming involved in the personal lives of strangers and giving them new life. That's love.

Jesus mentored His disciples who were everyday fishermen, tax collectors, accountants. They were anything but qualified carriers of His word, but they went on to change the world after He was gone from this earthly life.

I wonder if we could have contended with James and John, who were known as "Sons of Thunder" because of their fiery zeal and extreme reactions. Could we have loved and forgiven Peter, who continually promised that he would never leave Jesus and yet vehemently denied that he even knew Jesus? Peter had insisted he was ready to die for his Master! He had no idea the fear he would display when he was accused of being one of Jesus' followers.

Yet after Jesus was crucified, buried, and rose from the dead, He sent word to tell Peter that He was back. It doesn't stop there. Peter was the one who delivered his first sermon to thousands in Jerusalem on the day of Pentecost. Peter was changed from a coward running away from the crowds to a witness for Jesus after receiving the Holy Spirit. Love will change you when you allow His presence to rule and reign.

Father, as I face life's challenges, give me Your strength to rise up as a conqueror and give love to those in need. In Jesus' name, amen.

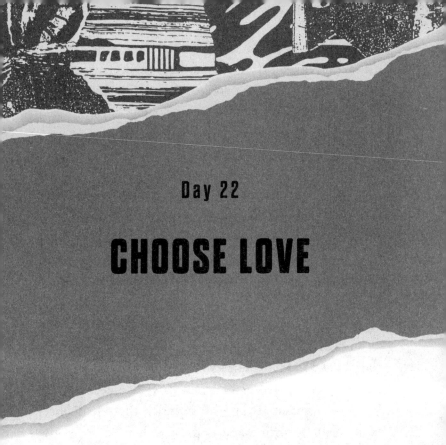

Day 22

CHOOSE LOVE

*Now I am giving you a new commandment:
Love each other. Just as I have loved you,
you should love each other. Your love for one
another will prove to the world that you are
my disciples.*

—John 13:34–35

L ove is one of the most overused and misunderstood
words in our vocabulary. I can "love" French fries or

a television program or maybe even "love" someone who makes me feel good when I'm around them. I'm sure this word is so confusing to people from other countries who are trying to learn the true meaning of *love* in the English language.

We must go to the Bible for an example of true love. Love started with God, and He continues to love us despite our sinful ways. God sent His only begotten Son to this earth as a defenseless baby to live and breathe for thirty-three years while giving us an example of true love. God's sacrifice of His Son gives each of us the chance to be righteous even though we don't deserve righteousness. It's amazing to realize I was so bad that God had to die for me, but I am so loved that He *wanted* to die for me.

If God chose to love me when I was so undeserving, then I need to follow His example and love others as He loved me. He loved Peter when Peter denied Him. He loved the woman at the well so much that He deliberately went through Samaria to meet her. He loved the young men who became His disciples long before they had anything going for them. Jesus loved the outcasts, the rejected, the lepers, the demon-possessed, and the scorned. He loved us all and He died for us all. He gave us the example of true love. It's now up to us to walk out that love.

Father, give me insight into true love as I walk out Your love and forgiveness in my daily life. In Jesus' name, amen.

Day 23

RELEASE YOUR ROAR

On the day of Pentecost all the believers
were meeting together in one place.
Suddenly, there was a sound from heaven
like the roaring of a mighty windstorm, and
it filled the house where they were sitting.

—Acts 2:1–2

Jesus instructed His disciples to wait in Jerusalem until
they were baptized with the Holy Spirit. Ten days

59

after Jesus ascended into heaven, they were waiting in the upper room in Jerusalem, praying constantly with the other believers. *Suddenly* there was a sound; however, we know "suddenly" took ten days of their coming together in one accord. These people were convinced of the truth of who Jesus was and were determined to make His purpose known. When the time came for the Spirit to descend, His coming was not a gradual process but a sudden intervention from heaven. The gushing wind was heard by all while the "tongues of fire" (Acts 2:3) that rested on each of them was personal.

Thousands were in the streets to celebrate the Passover when these believers came stumbling down in the early morning, filled with the Holy Spirit. This presented a great opportunity for the disciples to testify of the Lord's resurrection and power. When the multitudes heard Peter rise up with authority and give the message of deliverance, their hearts were pierced and three thousand were baptized that day. Peter, who had been full of fear and would not stand up as Jesus' follower before His death, now, full of the Holy Spirit, released a roar that is still being heard throughout the world today.

Father, I want to release a roar that will serve my generation and generations to come. Give me the wisdom to know when to speak and what to say. In Jesus' name, amen.

Day 24

IT'S NEVER TOO LATE

Peter's words pierced their hearts, and
they said to him and to the other apostles,
"Brothers, what should we do?"

—Acts 2:37

Today's verse happened on the day of Pentecost when
the Holy Spirit was poured out on the 120 followers

of Jesus Christ who had been waiting in the upper room in Jerusalem for ten days as Jesus had instructed them to do after the crucifixion (Acts 1:4). As the Holy Spirit fell upon them, they began speaking in different languages that were understood by the multitudes who had gathered in the city for Pentecost.

Peter began delivering his first sermon to the thousands who would help birth the church. Their hearts were pierced as he described the love of Jesus Christ and how He gave His life for fallen man so that anyone who repented could have eternal life. That day about three thousand people were baptized and began a new journey with the Savior.

Whenever I read the book of Acts, I remember a certain night in my upstairs bedroom at my mom and dad's home. If you had told me I had strayed too far from mercy to receive grace, I would have easily believed you. However, as I cried out to God for the first time in my life, I knew He answered my cry. I surrendered my everything to Him. That night I knew in my spirit that God was ready for me to make a life change. After thirty-nine years of indecision, all it took was for me to realize it wasn't too late for change.

Jesus Christ loved me despite my faults and failures. When I said that I did not know how to forgive others, Jesus let me know that forgiveness is a conscious decision. He let me know that forgiveness is an ongoing process that happens every day. Just because you forgive once doesn't mean you will never have to forgive again. When pain surfaces, forgive again.

Father, as I remember how You forgive me daily, allow me to extend that same forgiveness to others. Help me model Your ways as I make amends to those I've hurt and offer forgiveness to those who have injured me. In Jesus' name, amen.

MAKE AN IMPACT

*In Joppa there was a disciple named
Tabitha (in Greek her name is
Dorcas); she was always doing good
and helping the poor.*
—ACTS 9:36 NIV

We don't know the history of Tabitha—whether she
had a husband or children or if she was rich or poor.

We do know, however, that she made an impact wherever she went. One of the major ways she helped others was by sewing robes and other clothing for the poor.

Tabitha was compassionate and kind. She was an important part of the community. When she died suddenly, everyone mourned the loss of such a wonderful friend. Normally in the Jewish community, the dead were buried soon after death, but Tabitha's body was placed in an upper room as Christians sprang into action. They knew Peter was nearby performing healing miracles. The community sent two men to persuade Peter to come and pray for Tabitha. Faith was building that this woman, a disciple of Jesus, would be raised from the dead.

As Peter arrived, the mourning widows began showing him all the clothing Dorcas had made for them. Peter could have consoled these women and gone on with his business, but he sensed a different purpose for being at this place at this time. He began to pray, and Tabitha opened her eyes and sat up. The news spread through the whole town, and many believed in the Lord (Acts 9:39–42).

Tabitha had obeyed Jesus' command to clothe the poor and care for the widows. She devoted herself to those in need and had a tremendous impact upon her community.

This story covers only seven verses, yet it contains a powerful reminder of the impact we can have on our communities.

Father, give me the ability in the Spirit to understand Your desire for my life. I want to fulfill Your purpose and plan. In Jesus' name, amen.

Day 26

CHOOSE TO BE HAPPY

A cheerful heart is good medicine,
but a broken spirit saps a person's strength.
—Proverbs 17:22

The biblical character Joseph suffered great loss, but he kept a cheerful heart despite his circumstances. Joseph's brothers sold him into slavery, and he was thrown into prison for a crime he had not committed. When he was reunited with his brothers, they were afraid that Joseph would hold their crime against them; however, he not only forgave them but blessed them with an abundance of food for their families. He told them that what they intended for harm, the Lord had turned to good. He looked for joy in his situation and was blessed tremendously. "Until the time came to fulfill his dreams, the LORD tested Joseph's character" (Psalm 105:19).

As I struggled to become the mom my boys needed in our time of less than, I turned to God for forgiveness for all the hurt I had allowed and asked Him for direction for my next season. I turned my mourning into dancing, and I chose to enter my place of employment with a cheerful heart. I was able to change the atmosphere wherever I was placed. I learned that a cheerful heart is much more important than fleeting riches.

Like my dad would say when a brother fell, "His character could not keep up with his platform." He continually told me to check my heart. If God tested Joseph's character, I know that God will be testing my character for my next season of advancement too.

I choose to walk in joy and peace. I choose to stand in forgiveness. I choose to love others despite themselves. I choose to be happy where I'm planted. Get unstuck, make the same choices, and soar!

Father, I will allow joy and peace to be my constants in my life seasons. Give me the strength to love others despite pain and to choose joy over grief. In Jesus' name, amen.

CHOOSE YOUR TRIBE

Some men came carrying a paralyzed man on a sleeping mat. They tried to take him inside to Jesus, but they couldn't reach him because of the crowd. So they went up to the roof and took off some tiles. Then they lowered the sick man on his mat down into the crowd, right in front of Jesus. Seeing their faith, Jesus said to the man, "Young man, your sins are forgiven."

—LUKE 5:18–20

Four friends in Capernaum heard that Jesus was in town and wanted to carry their paralyzed friend to Him to be healed. When they arrived at the house where Jesus was speaking, there was no way to get another person inside, so his friends carried him to the roof and began removing tiles. They lowered their friend through the hole in the roof, and Jesus was so impressed by their faith that He immediately forgave the man's sins and healed him on the spot. We all need "crazy" friends who will do whatever is necessary to assist us in getting our breakthrough.

This paralyzed man could never have gotten to Jesus alone. He needed a tribe who believed that he could be healed and then figured out a way to get him where he needed to be. They decided to do whatever was necessary to see their friend touched by the man Christ Jesus.

Many people would have given up. They could have said, "Maybe we'll try the next time Jesus comes through Capernaum." They could have waited outside, hoping to catch a glimpse of Jesus as He came out of the house. These men were radical in believing that if they could get their friend into Jesus' presence, he would be healed.

Choose your tribe—the people who will walk through life seasons with you—wisely.

Father, thank You for friends who are there when I need them. Give me the insight to choose wisely those who will be my tribe. In Jesus' name, amen.

Day 28

CLARITY

*Open my eyes to see
the wonderful truths in your
instructions.*
—Psalm 119:18

My favorite verse changes from time to time. For example, there was a time when my favorite verse was Psalm 37:23: "The steps of a good man are ordered by the Lord, and He delights in his way" (NKJV). I quoted this often, yet there were times I felt that my steps were not ordered by the Lord. I could not understand why life was so uncertain when the Lord was ordering my steps, and I could not seem to stand firm in my decisions.

Why was life so tough when the Lord was delighting in my way? Surely He wasn't delighting in the frustrations, hurt, and pain caused by those who were betraying me or gossiping about me. How could His Word be so opposite to what I was feeling? I felt I should be able to stand against the wiles of the devil and be motivated to face each day in a joyful manner as I faced life's challenges.

As I was praying one day, it was as though I had a visitation from the Lord, giving me a picture of this verse. I saw my garden with beautiful flowers and stepping stones laid out with a path to walk through and admire God's creation. I then saw myself running through the garden and, instead of stepping on the stones laid out for my benefit and the benefit of the beautiful flowers, I was missing every other stone and stepping on the flowers instead.

God explained that He had laid out the steps I was to take but, in my own selfish way, I had determined I would walk wherever I desired. I realized we can only live the life He purposed for us if we stay on track, seeking to understand His Word.

Father, as I read Your Word daily, give me the insight and understanding as to why You have given me the Bible to determine my steps. In Jesus' name, amen.

When God shows you
something, don't dismiss it.
It's clarity you prayed for,
not confusion.

—RTK

Day 29

DO WHAT NO ONE ELSE WANTS TO DO

*I, John, am your brother and your partner
in suffering and in God's Kingdom and in
the patient endurance to which Jesus calls
us. I was exiled to the island of Patmos
for preaching the word of God and for my
testimony about Jesus.*

—REVELATION 1:9

The apostle John wrote the book of Revelation when he
was banished to the island of Patmos, which was called

a "sterile" island because no vegetation was able to grow there. Because this island was rocky, barren, and desolate, the Roman government used it as a place for criminals. It was no picnic to be sentenced to this barren place.

John wasn't guilty of defrauding the government or breaking any law except piercing the hearts of those who did not believe in Jesus Christ. The Romans knew he'd never change his belief system. Maybe he would starve to death or eventually realize he couldn't change their beliefs. Yet John survived. Because John had the courage to stand firm against the odds, we have the book of Revelation.

I cannot even imagine being on that island with hardened criminals—no green growth of any sort, scarcely enough food to keep a man alive—yet John lived to tell his story. He did whatever it took to stay alive and to hear God's voice.

We all go through times when we feel deserted, beaten down, and unable to face our next challenge. Then we get a second breath, and we get up one more time than we fall down. If you want success, you must do what others are unwilling to do. John was on the isle of Patmos, serving his sentence and waiting for God to change his dynamic.

Father, give me the insight and determination to get up one more time than I fall down. I want to receive revelation of Your Spirit and understanding of Your power. In Jesus' name, amen.

DON'T BE INTIMIDATED

Stay alert! Watch out for your great enemy,
the devil. He prowls around like a roaring
lion, looking for someone to devour.
—1 PETER 5:8

As I meditate on today's scripture, I envision the enemy prowling around, trying to cause me to cower in his presence. He comes as a roaring lion but without the strength of the lion. He is looking for someone he can take down—someone who doesn't understand that when we have the Holy Spirit as a weapon, we can easily defeat him.

When we understand that our weapons are mighty through God for pulling down strongholds and casting down all imaginations, we can get unstuck, rise up, and claim the territory that has been promised.

When you become a child of God, you take on His name and His power. He fills you with His presence unlike anyone in the Old Testament experienced. They were blessed with visitations from God; however, since the day of Pentecost we have had the privilege of being filled with the Holy Spirit. We can carry His presence with us wherever we go.

The enemy's goal is to paralyze you and weaken you from the inside out. Fear is one of his favorite weapons, so he uses fear to block your faith. James tells us to submit to God and resist the devil, and the devil will flee from us (4:7). *Submit* means to yield to the authority of another. When you submit you are letting God know that you are yielding to His will. You are walking by faith when there are financial crises, sickness, and even death. You will not allow the enemy to claim the territory given you by God.

Stand your ground, take back all that's been lost, and expect new territories to open up today.

Father, I submit my life, my family, and my tomorrows into Your care, and I stand on Your promises that are "yes" and "amen." In Jesus' name, amen.

DON'T MISS YOUR MOMENT

> *If you keep quiet at a time like this, deliverance*
> *and relief for the Jews will arise from some*
> *other place, but you and your relatives will die.*
> *Who knows if perhaps you were made queen*
> *for just such a time as this?*
> —Esther 4:14

Esther, orphaned as a child, was raised by her cousin Mordecai, who became like a father to her. As she came of age, Esther was chosen from among the young women of the kingdom to compete to become the next queen to King Xerxes. His former queen, Queen Vashti, angered him when he summoned her to present herself before the nobles during a feast and she refused. She was removed from her position as queen and banished from the king's presence. A royal decree went out that a new queen would be chosen in her place. As Mordecai prepared his cousin to be presented before the king, he insisted that Esther not reveal her Jewish identity to King Xerxes, as it could endanger her family and she might not be selected as queen.

Esther heeded his advice and was selected to be the new queen.

When Haman, a court official, threatened the fate of all the Jews in the land, Mordecai knew Queen Esther could influence the king to favor the Jews. Mordecai suggested that she go to the king about the possible annihilation of the Jews, but Esther was hesitant and afraid. What if the king did not receive her or believe her? She could be killed! But her cousin reminded her of the purpose God might have intended for her life in enabling her, of all the women Xerxes could have chosen, to have risen in esteem and been selected as queen. Mordecai reminded her that God's people, the Jews, would triumph with or without her, but perhaps God had set her in position for this moment in time. Read the full story of Esther. It's short and reads like a real-life mystery.

We each have a purpose and a plan "for such a time as

this." Act on those moments and then watch God come through for you.

———

Father, when I am faced with my moment, give me the grace to stand and do the right thing. In Jesus' name, amen.

POWERFUL, NOT PITIFUL

For God has not given us a spirit of fear and timidity, but of power, love, and self-discipline.
—2 TIMOTHY 1:7

We are born self-centered with a desire to protect our egos and our rights. When we feel we are not being treated as we should, self-pity is the result. We sulk and obsess over our hurts, which easily destroys relationships that are important to God. We are still living out the sin of the first couple in the garden of Eden. Adam and Eve felt they deserved more. So they ate of the fruit of the Tree of Knowledge of Good and Evil. When self is dominant, as with Adam and Eve, God is not. You cannot be powerful when you are pitiful.

King Ahab is another example of self-centeredness. As he looked over at Naboth's garden, King Ahab began to sulk because he coveted the garden and wanted to buy it (1 Kings 21). Jezebel, King Ahab's wife, set a plan in motion to take Naboth's garden, the only property he owned. Only after the plan was carried out, which resulted in Naboth's death, was King Ahab happy. Reading on, we know that powerful King Ahab became powerless, and his entire dynasty was eventually destroyed.

It's so easy to get stuck in the mundane when we believe we deserve more than we're getting. We can feel stuck when it seems we've done everything possible to bring about change, yet change doesn't happen. We may see others passing us in promotions and financial achievements and wonder why our prayers haven't been answered. We can easily lose sight of the good things in our lives. We can choose to be content and joyful or allow negativity to rob us of what has been promised us.

Father, help me to be content with the life You have given me, and give me the insight to choose joy and contentment. In Jesus' name, amen.

Day 33

DON'T OVERTHINK

*When Ahab got home, he told Jezebel everything
Elijah had done, including the way he had killed all
the prophets of Baal. So Jezebel sent this message to
Elijah: "May the gods strike me and even kill me if
by this time tomorrow I have not killed you just as
you killed them."*

—1 Kings 19:1–2

God's chosen people, the Israelites, had turned their back on Him. King Ahab and his wife, Jezebel, had erected altars to the false god Baal, and the Israelites were worshipping him. God sent the prophet Elijah to announce a coming drought that lasted more than three years. Elijah proposed a challenge on Mount Carmel to prove the power of God against the false gods. After the 450 false prophets cried out to their gods and nothing happened, Elijah called on the true God, who sent fire from heaven. Then Elijah killed all the false prophets, according to God's instructions.

The people were amazed and fell face down to worship Elijah's God. After Elijah prayed and God sent a rainstorm, the Israelites turned back toward God. Jezebel, who had not gone to the showdown at Mount Carmel, was furious when she heard the outcome. She threatened Elijah's life.

We would expect Elijah to laugh at Jezebel's threats since he had just seen God send fire from heaven. He saw God deliver the false prophets into his hand, and he heard the entire nation of Israel praise God as they repented. However, he became afraid and ran away. Elijah allowed his mind to process the what-ifs, and he gave up. He told the Lord he would rather die than go any farther. After all the amazing things that God had done for Elijah, he was focusing on one woman's threats.

We all become discouraged, and sometimes we fail. But God does not leave us. He gives us the opportunity to repent and draw close to Him. God's plans cannot be stopped. It just may take a while longer to get where we're supposed to be. Don't overthink the process.

———

Father, give me the understanding to move when You speak. Help me stay in Your Word so I can have the mind of Christ. In Jesus' name, amen.

Day 34

EXPOSE YOUR POSITIVES

She would sit under the Palm of Deborah, between Ramah and Bethel in the hill country of Ephraim, and the Israelites would go to her for judgment.

—JUDGES 4:5

Deborah is the only female judge mentioned in the book of Judges. One of the most influential women in the Bible, Deborah is a great example of God calling ordinary people to do extraordinary things. She would sit under the palm tree in the hill country of Ephraim as the children of Israel came to her for wisdom.

When Israel was threatened by the might of King Jabin of Canaan, the Israelites turned to Deborah. She summoned Barak, an able military leader, to lead Israel against the Canaanite army. At first Barak was reluctant to enter into battle with King Jabin. He knew the Canaanites had superior military technology and nine hundred chariots. Barak knew his citizen militia were fewer in number, comparatively untrained, and had inferior weapons. This mighty warrior told Deborah he would not fight unless Deborah went with him. Barak knew Deborah had a connection with God and they would need that connection. Deborah agreed but told Barak the honor of victory over Jabin's army would not go to him because the Lord would deliver the Canaanites' commander, Sisera, into the hands of a woman.

During the battle, Sisera realized he was losing to the children of Israel because God had thrown Sisera's military force into confusion, so he fled on foot. He went to the tent of Jael, the wife of Heber, because of an alliance between King Jabin and Heber's family. He had no idea that Heber had kinship ties with the Israelites. Heber was descended from Jethro who had been Moses' father-in-law.

After Jael gave Sisera food and a place to rest, she pounded a tent peg through his temple as he slept. The story doesn't tell us what prompted Jael to kill Sisera. Whatever it was, the Israelites celebrated her as a national heroine.

Deborah's story would not be complete without acknowledging Jael, who stepped up to stake her claim in history and expose her positives. She was at the right place at the right time and did what she knew she had to do.

———

Father, help me rise up and do what I need to do at the right time. Assist me in accomplishing the great feats You have already ordered for me before I was even born. In Jesus' name, amen.

Day 35

FIGHT FOR YOUR LIFE

We are human, but we don't wage war as humans do. We use God's mighty weapons, not worldly weapons, to knock down the strongholds of human reasoning and to destroy false arguments.
—2 Corinthians 10:3–4

A violent war is raging around each of us twenty-four hours a day. It's the battle for our minds, and the enemy never takes a break. This battle is so intense because our greatest asset is our minds.

If the enemy can silence us, he has won the war. It is up to us to understand we have weapons of warfare that will help us. Our weapons are mighty for pulling down strongholds in the spirit realm. The enemy wins when we do not understand our power.

The apostle Paul told us we can knock down the strongholds of human reasoning; however, we must understand that a stronghold is a mental block. It's anything that comes against the kingdom of God and His righteousness. It can be believing in the systems of this world over the power of God or seeking the approval of others.

We are to bring our thoughts into captivity so the enemy cannot reign in our personal lives. Paul wrote that he did not understand himself: He wanted to do good, but he didn't. He seemed to do what he hated. He understood that, in his sinful nature, he did all the wrong things (Romans 7).

Have you been there? You know what you are supposed to be doing, yet you sin anyway. It's a fight for your life, and the enemy will never stop until he wins. When you give up that sin and allow Jesus Christ to be Lord of your life, even your mind must submit to His will.

Father, as I humble myself in submission to You, I lay my desires at the cross and choose to pick up my spiritual weapons to war against the enemy. In Jesus' name, amen.

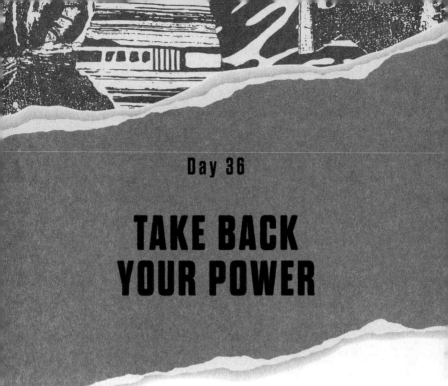

TAKE BACK YOUR POWER

Do not let any part of your body become an instrument of evil to serve sin. Instead, give yourselves completely to God, for you were dead, but now you have new life. So use your whole body as an instrument to do what is right for the glory of God.

—ROMANS 6:13

Virtually every battle with sin that you fight will be lost or won in your human reasoning. Your thought life is not a playground but a battlefield, and the stakes are high. The weapons on this battlefield are spiritual and mental, not physical or martial. You will never win this battle until you determine to take back your power. That power comes from recognizing that Jesus is Lord over this entire world and you are but a warrior waiting for His call.

In today's scripture, the writer, Paul, ushers you onto a battlefield where you are not to let any part of your body become an instrument of evil to serve sin. You will use your entire body to overcome sin and enjoy the blessings of your salvation, or you will allow the gray matter housed between your two ears to determine you cannot win in this life. The call is yours to make.

Realize today that you are where your thoughts have brought you, and that you will go tomorrow where your thoughts lead you. There is a system within our bodies called the reticular activating system (or RAS); this system tells us that we will become what we think about most of the time. When you become a Christian, God does a miracle within your spirit. You've been forgiven of your sins and have taken on a brand-new nature. That does not mean you automatically become perfect in this life.

Following your conversion, your mind has to be renewed, and the battle begins. However, you don't have to do it alone. God gives you the power to change. Think about this quote from Ralph Waldo Emerson: "Sow a thought, reap an action. Sow an action, reap a habit. Sow a habit, reap character. Sow character, reap a destiny."

Father, give me the power to use all You have given me to be used up for Your glory. In Jesus' name, amen.

Day 37

IF YOU BELIEVE IT, YOU WILL SEE IT

*I tell you, you can pray for anything, and
if you believe that you've received it, it will
be yours.*

—MARK 11:24

I grew up on testimonies of faith because my parents
first had been evangelists and then church planters and
pastors. My brother and I often rode in the back seat of
our car, headed with our parents to a hospital in downtown Atlanta to pray for the sick. Probably one of the

most unusual facts about our family is that we never had babysitters. My parents always wanted us with them, whether we were climbing Stone Mountain or having an all-night prayer service.

Even the early morning prayer gatherings included our being dragged along with our blankets to the church to join the saints of God as everyone prayed for revival. I assumed everyone's family was the same as mine until I grew up and realized not all families were centered around church activities as ours was. The result was that, even in my times of crisis, I found my way back to God because our parents taught us that if you believe it, you will see it. I now believe for anything and everything.

Have you ever inspected a mustard seed? It is so small you can hardly pick it up with your fingers, and yet we read in the Bible that if our faith is even that size, we can see miracles. Scripture tells us we can even say to a mountain to move from here to there, and it will move (Matthew 17:20–21). It's all about faith.

Your faith is meant to grow. It can only grow if you sow the right seeds in good soil. I'm not talking about a garden here. I'm talking about spending time each day in God's Word and watching it produce astronomical faith. Just believe and watch God do the rest.

Father, give me the faith to believe that all things are possible because I trust You and receive Your Word. In Jesus' name, amen.

Day 38

YOU ARE QUALIFIED

It is not that we think we are qualified to do anything on our own. Our qualification comes from God.

—2 CORINTHIANS 3:5

As a child in elementary school, I was labeled "learning disabled." From the first grade until high school, I struggled with word comprehension. I never could grasp phonics and always felt like a failure. I watched my brother come home after school, throw his books on the table, and run out to play because he had finished his homework at school. I knew my afternoons and evenings would be spent sitting with my mom, rehearsing spelling words until I was sick of them.

I would get up the next morning and my mom would do her best to coach me into remembering what I had studied. But the words were just not there. I didn't understand why life was so difficult, and I certainly couldn't have imagined my present life, ministering to people around the world and pouring into their hurts, habits, and hang-ups. I realize now that God took my mess and turned it into a message. The girl who could not remember words from one day to the next now quotes hundreds of scriptures from memory and flows seamlessly during interviews because God has qualified her for this time.

When the rulers, religious leaders, and religion scholars in Jerusalem questioned Peter and John about healing a crippled man, they explained that it came because of the name of Jesus Christ. He was the One who qualified them (Acts 4). It was not of their own education, might, or strength that they performed miracles. These uneducated apostles were called by God and qualified to do the work of ministry. I get it. I, too, could never accomplish the work of ministry without Jesus in my life. If He calls you, He will qualify you.

━━━━━

Father, as I live each day to serve You, give me the grace to walk out the purpose that You have already planned for me. In Jesus' name, amen.

Day 39

IMAGINE MORE

Now all glory to God, who is able, through his mighty power at work within us, to accomplish infinitely more than we might ask or think.

—Ephesians 3:20

I lived with labels throughout my childhood as I wandered from distraction to distraction. I had a learning problem and could never seem to measure up to those in my life who meant so much to me. My older brother, Rob, seemed like a genius to me as a child, because he never studied yet always made the mark. I, in turn, remember my mother always at my side, insisting that I could understand phonics, that I could measure up to my classmates. Yet I couldn't. Why me? Why was I destined to be a failure? That was my daily internal conversation.

Then I realized I could make an impression by being a social butterfly. If there was a party, everyone wanted to invite me because I could make things happen. I always tried to turn everyone's attention away from the real issues of life to just having fun. Before I had a driver's license, there were numerous friends waiting to pick me up on Friday nights when everyone was going out. I just had to choose who I wanted to ride with. I thought if life had dealt me a serious blow, I would make it pay and have fun doing it. I lived this way until I was thirty-six, with two sons and a failed marriage. I had to face reality and understand that parties and hard living would not pay the bills nor keep my family together.

At thirty-six I began to develop a true relationship with Jesus Christ as my Lord and Savior. The past eleven years of my life have culminated into a life that I could never have imagined, yet I now imagine more, more, more. I continually dream of new ventures I can conquer and then watch them succeed. From broken and destitute to a millionaire in eleven years! From losing a company to owning numerous businesses and pastoring the greatest church, I spend my days dreaming and walking out those dreams. You, too, can become what you imagine.

Imagine more!

Father, give me wisdom today to imagine the greatness that comes with serving You. I want to be the best me I can be. In Jesus' name, amen.

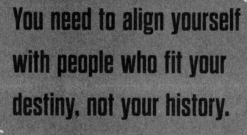

You need to align yourself
with people who fit your
destiny, not your history.
—RTK

Day 40

IT REALLY DOESN'T MATTER

Then the devil said to him, "If you are the Son of God, tell this stone to become a loaf of bread."

—Luke 4:3

After John baptized Jesus in the Jordan River, Jesus was led into the desert to be tempted by the devil. After forty days the enemy told Jesus to prove who He was—to prove He was the Son of God. Jesus refused and essentially said, "I don't have to prove anything to anyone. My Father announced who I was." Jesus let the enemy know that it really didn't matter who he thought Jesus was. He was who God said He was.

I wonder how many times we allow the enemy to steal our focus because we're trying desperately to prove our worth. It starts when we're small children trying to stand up to bullies, and it becomes natural to live as if we're constantly struggling to show the world who we really are.

We cannot know our true worth until we understand the tremendous sacrifice made for us by our Lord Jesus Christ when He went to the cross, sinless but representing every sin that had ever or would ever be committed. It really doesn't matter what anyone thinks of you if you know who you are; you were created to be one of a kind, and there will never be another like you.

God created each of us to be unique. Modern technology understands this. You probably know your fingerprints cannot be duplicated, but did you know that even your brain cells are unique? Take time today to be thankful for the amazing human that is wrapped in your flesh, called by your name, and made in the image of the great God of this universe.

Father, I give You honor and thanks today for creating me one of a kind and giving me a distinct purpose to do Your will. In Jesus' name, amen.

Day 41

GOD HAS A PLAN

"For I know the plans I have for you," says the LORD. *"They are plans for good and not for disaster, to give you a future and a hope. In those days when you pray, I will listen. If you look for me wholeheartedly, you will find me."*
—JEREMIAH 29:11–13

I remember years ago sitting in a ladies' meeting listening to my mother talking about the importance of hearing God's voice. This was during my wild-oats season when I had no connection to the spirit realm. My mother said it was of ultimate importance that Deborah, as a judge in Israel, be attentive to God's voice. She was not only a woman in leadership, but she was speaking into the lives of everyone who needed her wisdom.

A lady at the meeting quoted Jeremiah 29:11. Jeremiah was speaking to the Jews in the midst of hardship and suffering, and they were desiring a quick change. God's response was not to provide an immediate escape; God knew the plans He had for them were for good and not disaster. His plans were to give them hope for their future.

Then we read verses 12 and 13 in which the Jews were promised that when they prayed God would listen if they searched for Him with all their hearts. These scriptures gave me comfort when I was so far from knowing who I was. His promise to me was that if I prayed and sought Him, He would allow me to find Him. Now, years later, I see the fruit of my searching and understand the importance of knowing Jesus Christ as Lord and Savior. I remember my dad singing, "When you've tried everything and everything has failed, try Jesus." I determined I would give God my present and my future. I wanted change, and He wanted my heart. He will give you whatever you need when you seek Him and find Him.

Father, as I humble myself before You, I want change. I want stability. I want peace. I give You my present and my future. In Jesus' name, amen.

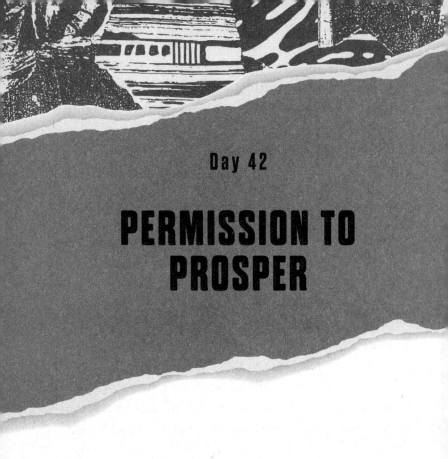

PERMISSION TO PROSPER

Those who listen to instruction will prosper;
*those who trust the L*ORD *will be joyful.*
—PROVERBS 16:20

I remember a young woman, about eighteen years old, who lived in a world of make-believe. She was always dreaming of bigger cars and fine homes, a wardrobe full of labels representing the rich and famous. She lived in a world of comparison—comparing her present life to those who had already "arrived." Yes, I am sharing a certain season in my life.

I was raised in a pastor's home. If there happened to be a week with more than enough, my dad always knew a family who needed it more than we did. I watched him "squander," as I interpreted it, our income on everyone else, while we wanted a fine life like other pastors' kids I knew. Why did their families vacation regularly and shop designer labels, when my mom was always pinching pennies and buying sale items?

As I grew older and began making a lucrative income, I determined to have the best, the latest in designs, and the biggest house. So I did. However, the latest and greatest did not solve my communication problems with my spouse, whom I adored. It took me losing everything and moving back into my parents' home, which I had tried desperately to escape, to realize that money couldn't solve all our problems.

Proverbs 16:20 says that when we listen to instruction, we will prosper; when we trust God, we will be joyful. I can tell you that after submitting my entire being to Jesus Christ, He gave me the power to prosper. Walking in a season of prosperity and joy means so much more to me today than when I thought money solved everything.

God gives you permission to prosper; however, remember that you must first listen to His instruction. Know His will for you and allow Him to be Lord today.

Father, as I arise daily to go about my life and working for my income, give me the wisdom to make godly decisions as I allow You to be Lord. In Jesus' name, amen.

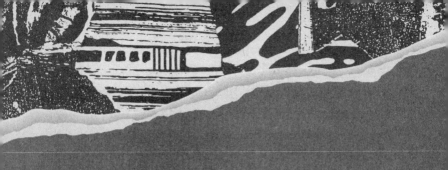

Day 43

JUST START

"But forget all that—
　　it is nothing compared to what I am
　　　　going to do.
For I am about to do something new.
　　See, I have already begun! Do you not
　　　　see it?
I will make a pathway through the
　　wilderness.
　　I will create rivers in the dry
　　　　wasteland."
　　　　　　—Isaiah 43:18–19

We often hear people instructing us to live in the present—to not dwell on the past. Yet because my past was so destructive, I look back and am so thankful that God brought me out of a mess to give me a message. I often look back to remember the girl who tried to do it all on her own. I understand now that God is the balance in the equation of my life.

No, I did not go to college to become an entrepreneur or preacher or motivational coach. I did try for a few days to be the model Bible school student that my parents dreamed I would become, but it just didn't work for me. I determined that I knew the best avenue for my life. I was eighteen years old and wanted out of my parents' house so badly that I thought marriage was the answer. I remember waking up in Mexico with my new husband in a one-bedroom apartment where my only view was a pile of garbage in the middle of the street. I could not speak a word of Spanish. I thought I was going to live out my dreams in this tropical paradise that turned into a nightmare from hell.

This was the beginning of a series of bad choices that determined my present. Our time in Mexico only lasted six months before we relocated back to the United States. I wish I could tell you that this decision was a wake-up call, but it would not end so quickly. My marriage lasted fourteen months, and then I did it again. No thoughts, no prayers, I just jumped into the next season. I realize now I was good at starting over. However, I could never seem to make the plan work. Finally, at age forty-nine I realized all the bad decisions had one person in the equation: me. I finally looked at me, went through deliverance, and broke many soul ties. I'm telling you my story so you can understand we all mess up, but we can get up again and again.

Just start your journey today and allow Jesus to be the Lord of your decisions—of your life.

━━━━━━━━

Father, help me be a good starter in my seasons to determine my tomorrows. I submit myself to You to be what You created me to be. In Jesus' name, amen.

Day 44

GET UP ONE MORE TIME

The godly may trip seven times, but they
will get up again.
But one disaster is enough to
overthrow the wicked.
—Proverbs 24:16

For the one who is doing right, failure is not the end of the road. It makes a difference how you are living when you fall. Proverbs 24:16 shows us a clear comparison between the just person who falls and the wicked who falls. The just person rises up to continue moving forward, but the wicked man can be overthrown by just one disaster. We all know that in this life there will be many misfortunes. It's up to us to determine how we manage those.

When someone has fallen in discouragement and disgrace, it's easy for others to decide that they must have been doing wrong or living in sin. The Bible says, however, that even someone living a righteous life before God will face failure.

As I lay broken and ashamed after marriage and business failures, I cried out to God to release me from my pain. I was not the righteous person who gets up after a disaster to move forward. I was guilty as charged, and I felt like everyone was judging me for my failures.

I remember God saying to me, *You must give your pain to Me.* I understood that the pain would not leave until I decided to get up and walk in forgiveness. My life changed, and I developed a relationship with Jesus Christ unlike anything I had ever experienced.

Have I fallen since that time? Absolutely! But I now have permanent access to God daily. Will I fall again? Probably. However, I now have the confidence to get up one more time than I fall down.

Father, help me understand how to get up one more time than I fall down. Give me the power to change myself and to assist those who walk with me. In Jesus' name, amen.

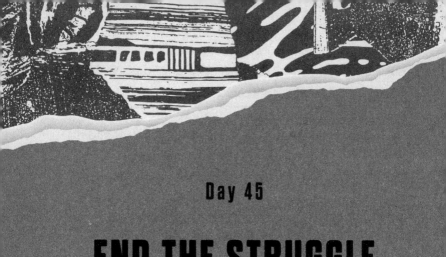

Day 45

END THE STRUGGLE

God saved you by his grace when you
believed. And you can't take credit for this;
it is a gift from God. Salvation is not a
reward for the good things we have done, so
none of us can boast about it.

—Ephesians 2:8–9

We meet people every day who are involved in the greatest struggle of their lives: whether to serve Jesus Christ or go through life without believing they have a need for salvation. Because I was raised in a pastor's home, my life centered around church and God's people. Yet as I matured into an adult, I began to make decisions that changed the course of my existence. I remember the day my mother was trying to encourage me because my husband and I were having a tough time. He had started drinking with his friends, and I felt unloved and unappreciated. His life was revolving around parties and his friends, so I decided to join in the party scene to make my marriage work. I told my mother that I did not want to live in a divided house, so I would change to make him happy. I had no idea that I was unlocking a party animal inside of me.

It was as though my life shifted on a downward spiral as I ended the struggle between doing what was right or doing what would keep my marriage together. If I could have seen ten years down the road, I would have never started the course of action that I lost control over.

My boys began going to sleep at night to "lullabies" of their parents screaming and fighting. I became the life of the party, and my friends didn't want to throw parties without Kimmie. I was fighting a war within myself because I knew my very existence was because of the grace of Jesus Christ. It took my marriage totally falling apart, losing my business, and losing my home to open my eyes to the truth of God's mercy.

There is always a struggle going on as you choose the God you will serve.

Look at me now. I made a choice to change, and you can too.

Father, thank You for never leaving nor forsaking me during my renegade life. All I want is to serve You with all that I am. In Jesus' name, amen.

Day 46

LET GO

"Don't sin by letting anger control you."
Don't let the sun go down while you are
still angry.

—EPHESIANS 4:26

Navigating through life's challenges often requires us to forgive and move on from our present circumstances. Letting go can be one of the hardest decisions you will ever make. I am a living, breathing example of brokenness who found solace in God, which changed my entire being from the inside out. My biggest problem was forgiving those who had hurt me throughout my childhood, teen years, and even into my adult years.

This wasn't just a temporary season; it continued through my entire life. I would move on from friendship to friendship, but the same rejection and discontentment followed me through each season. By the time I was thirty-six years old, recently separated from my sons' father and had lost my business, the most devastating event happened: moving back into my parents' home with my sons. It took me three years to determine I needed to file for a divorce and move on because there was no going back. I was in the middle of a letting-go crisis.

When I came face-to-face with the unforgiveness I had carried for so many years, I knew it was time to move on. But I could not seem to do this until I began letting go of people who had caused me pain. The evening I gave it all to God, He let me know I had to forgive and let go. It seemed like hours of remembering different people of influence throughout my life who had let me down, spoken ill against me, or rejected the girl I wanted to be. However, as I forgave each person, I experienced a peace unlike anything I had felt before.

Now I refuse to carry the heartache and pain of unforgiveness for even one day. It is easy for me to forgive, let go, and move on. I don't have to allow people who hurt me to be part of my life, but I do need to forgive and love them for Jesus' sake.

If Jesus could die for our sins by such a shameful death

on the cross, why can't we just forgive and move on? We have the perfect example to live by.

━━━━━━

Father, give me the strength to do whatever is necessary to live in forgiveness so I can let go and move on. In Jesus' name, amen.

Day 47

LEVEL UP

Jesus told him, "No! The Scriptures say,
'People do not live by bread alone,
but by every word that comes from the
mouth of God.'"
—MATTHEW 4:4

After moving back into my parents' home with my two boys, I had to come face-to-face with reality. I was middle-aged, financially ruined, a single mom, and definitely the black sheep of my family. My conversations with myself were always self-ridiculing, and I questioned every decision. Why would anyone want to hear what I had to say when I could not keep my family together, nor succeed with my business?

I was desperate for change. I finally realized that I needed God. I picked up my Bible and tried to read but nothing made sense to me. I could not remember Bible stories that had been read to me as a small child nor recall any of my Sunday school lessons. I was a pastor's daughter and never missed a Sunday, yet it was as though I had never been churched. I knew it was time for my life to change, and it was my responsibility to level up.

After purchasing a children's picture Bible, I began reading the stories as though my life depended on them. It did. The Bible stories, such as "David and the Giant," "The Three Hebrew Children in the Fiery Furnace," and "Daniel in the Lions' Den," all seemed new to me. It was as though I was reading these stories for the very first time. The children of Israel really did cross the Red Sea on dry ground! Amazing! I became so excited about learning the Bible stories that I waited anxiously through the workdays to return to my haven of safety in my bedroom at my parents' home so I could read.

How could I have known that the journey I was taking, the time I was spending on learning His Word, and the prayers that kept me grounded would bring me to the place I am today? I now know I cannot live by bread alone but by every word that comes from the mouth of God. I have learned hundreds of Scripture passages that I think about throughout the day. Doing so has enabled me to lead thousands on their journeys to freedom.

We call our experience with God personal because it requires one-on-one time with our heavenly Father. Take time today to allow Him to level you up.

Father, give me the desire to seek You and know You in a personal way. In Jesus' name, amen.

Day 48

MASTERPIECE

*For we are God's masterpiece. He has
created us anew in Christ Jesus, so we can
do the good things he planned for us long ago.*
—EPHESIANS 2:10

Surely not! How can a God who created this entire universe with the most amazing solar system of planets and
stars look at me and think I could be any more than I am:
a broken vessel unable to see the good that God sees in me?

If the enemy can keep those voices playing in your mind, he will keep you from soaring in this unstable world. How could I be called a masterpiece by the great Creator? How can He forgive me when I can't seem to forgive myself? Are you relating to the conversations played repeatedly through your mind as you try to focus on your good and not on your bad?

God has a plan for you: to do you good and not harm. He has a purpose for you and has already established your goings. It's up to you, however, to work with Him. The difference between your friend, Jesus Christ, and your enemy, the devil, is that Jesus is interested in all things working for your good.

Masterpiece means success, a gem, prize, treasure, and a piece of the Master. Do you understand how important you are to God? God loves what He created, so why shouldn't you? Why judge what God has called exquisite? Why take the blame for shame when Jesus has already taken your sins to the cross and now calls you righteous?

When you listen to His Word and not your thoughts, you will walk out success and fulfillment. You will see the vessel He created in you and allow Him to be Lord of your life. The sooner you see yourself for who you really are, the sooner you will take your position as His masterpiece.

Father, help me see the me that You created and give me the power to release the strength that is inside to do Your will. In Jesus' name, amen.

Day 49

LIGHTEN UP

A cheerful disposition is good for your health;
gloom and doom leave you bone-tired.
—PROVERBS 17:22 MSG

Sometimes we just need to lighten up. Had a good laugh lately? Or are you spending so much time trying to survive that you forget why you are living? Life isn't easy, but it's good to laugh a little even in your pain. Studies show that laughter can enhance physical and mental health. Laughter has a role in fighting viruses, bacteria, cancer, and disease. An article on stress management from the staff at the Mayo Clinic says that laughter not only helps in the short term by stimulating organs, activating and relieving your stress response, and soothing tension, it also improves your immune system, relieves pain, increases personal satisfaction, and improves your mood in the long term. I remember my dad saying that "'dis–ease' brings on disease."

When I was at my lowest, I wondered how I could celebrate any special days when I had failed my kids as a mom and taken away their security as a family unit. Then I realized that my kids wanted my presence more than they wanted presents. I had spent years working hard and trying to pacify those in my world who mattered to me, and I was miserable.

There was nothing left but my sons. And I still had to get up each day for them. I realized that if I had nothing else, I still had legacy. It was time to make decisions that would change our future. Holidays mean everything to me. They're not about the gifts we receive. They're about the time we invest in each other. Today I look at my boys, who have evolved into strong men who are sentimental about family, about home, about togetherness. We laugh a lot, we cry together, we hold each other in times of loss. We look forward to family outings—a Braves game, an evening downtown, or a movie. Anything to be together. All it took was for me to lighten up and realize that I had all I needed and more.

Father, as we live this life together, give my family insight into loving each other despite trials, wisdom to know when to be quiet, and opportunities to give away all that's been given to us. In Jesus' name, amen.

Day 50

LIKE YOURSELF

To acquire wisdom is to love yourself;
people who cherish understanding
will prosper.
—Proverbs 19:8

The world is fascinated with self. We're all concerned with who we are, what we are, and what we are trying to become. We can get so wrapped up in who we are that we forget the real reason God created us. God wanted relationship, so He created Adam and then provided the friend Adam needed. God took one of Adam's ribs to create a companion for Adam. Eve was the result. It was all about love.

God wants us to understand how much He loves us. It wasn't just about Adam and Eve and their relationship. God had us in mind as He set them in the garden of Eden. He wants a relationship with us. Not because He needs it, but because He loves us. To understand His love and build relationships with others, we must love what He created. To like yourself means you must take care of yourself. You must want to grow and become a responsible, contributing member of society. Quiet the negative voices telling you that you're not good enough, not smart enough, not worthy enough—just not enough.

It's pretty easy to see that your feelings about yourself can determine how you treat others. Do you stand in front of the mirror and criticize what God has created? Do you talk negatively to yourself when you make mistakes? Are you your harshest judge? When God told us to love our neighbors as ourselves, He knew we were fighting a battle to not only love ourselves but to just like what He had created. When we think of ourselves as God created us to be, it becomes easier to accept and like others as God created them to be.

Just as gardeners tend their plants with care, we should nurture our souls through self-compassion and the pursuit of wisdom. It is important to remember that self-worth and self-love are foundational to our overall happiness and success. We cannot like—let alone love—others until we like ourselves.

━━━━━━━━

Father, help me see the me You created me to be. Give me insight into the love You have for me so I can begin to love like You love. In Jesus' name, amen.

NO EXCUSES

The LORD asked Cain, "Where is your brother? Where is Abel?"

"I don't know," Cain responded. "Am I my brother's guardian?"

—GENESIS 4:9

Cain and Abel were the first two sons of Adam and Eve. Cain was a farmer, while Abel was a shepherd. When harvest came, Cain brought the Lord a gift from the crops he had grown, and Abel also brought the Lord a gift—an offering of blood, the best parts of the firstborn lambs of his flock. Both brothers made sacrifices to God, but God accepted only Abel's offering.

Many assume that the difference between their offerings was the reason God did not accept Cain's, but grain offerings were acceptable before God, though not as an atonement for sin. Cain's offering was rejected because of his heart's condition. This made Cain jealous of his brother and angry that God would accept his brother's sacrifice before his own. He killed Abel out of jealousy and anger.

Cain should have known better than to kill his brother; however, he was driven by his emotions and allowed anger to push him to commit this vicious act. God told Cain before he murdered his brother that "sin [was] crouching at the door" (Genesis 4:7), and it was up to Cain to rule over it. He was to subdue his sin and be its master. There is no record before this incident that Cain had been taught right and wrong, yet God expected Cain to do what was right. This began a lifetime of excuses for Cain.

We reach for excuses far too often. We hate to be reminded that our excuses are explaining away laziness, failure, giving up, or self-doubt. Our excuses drive us to failure because they let us take the easy way out. We all have things we could blame for derailing us in life. It's only after we identify the excuses we are using that we can really get ahead.

As I rehearse the story of my failures, I do my best to

honestly acknowledge that it took two to destroy my marriages. My exes were not the only ones to blame for the demise of marriage and family. I refuse to allow excuses to cloud my judgment as I enter the Lord's presence for forgiveness. Even in our failures, God has made a way for us through His Son, Jesus Christ. Redemption is free to those who earnestly seek His forgiveness and refuse to make excuses.

Father, I confess every sin that I have committed against You as I receive Your forgiveness for my transgressions. In Jesus' name, amen.

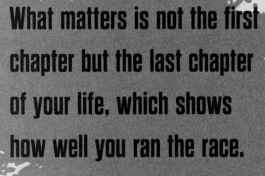

What matters is not the first chapter but the last chapter of your life, which shows how well you ran the race.

—RTK

NO STORM TOO STRONG

Suddenly, a fierce storm struck the lake, with waves breaking into the boat. But Jesus was sleeping. The disciples went and woke him up, shouting, "Lord, save us! We're going to drown!"

—Matthew 8:24–25

The significance of Jesus calming the storm is pertinent to our daily lives as we face numerous types of storms.

Sickness, divorce, pain, or financial hardships are just a few storms that many families face.

The Sea of Galilee is known for sudden storms. The disciples were seasoned fishermen, and we would expect them to be prepared for any weather crisis. However, they totally lost control as a furious storm blew in and fear gripped them. Jesus was with them, but He was asleep. The storm did not even bother or awaken him.

Jesus was on a mission. He was on His way to a demon-possessed man on the other side. He had faith that God would see Him to the other side, so He slept. When the disciples woke Him, He immediately asked about their faith. Jesus saw fear in their eyes and wondered why they would allow such fear to rule them when He was there. Then He rebuked the wind and waves and calmed the storm. The disciples were in awe that even the storm obeyed His command.

We, too, can use these examples to instill faith as we face our own storms. We are promised that He will not leave us nor forsake us, so why feel alone when we are shaken? My greatest comfort when faced with a crisis is to remember what Jesus Christ has already done for me. I look back at victories and then look ahead in faith that He will do what He promised.

Father, as darkness overwhelms me in the storm, give me the strength to get up one more time and know that You will bring me through. In Jesus' name, amen.

Day 53

NO WORRIES

So don't worry about tomorrow, for
tomorrow will bring its own worries.
Today's trouble is enough for today.

—Matthew 6:34

You feel a lump. You just know it's cancer. You receive a letter from the IRS. You just know you're being audited. You answer a strange phone call. You just know your spouse is having an affair.

How often do you allow worries about the unknown to sap your daily strength to the point that you cannot even accomplish that day's tasks? Your enemy, the devil, will do whatever necessary to make sure you never accomplish the purpose written for you by God as He knitted you together in your mother's womb. There is no way you can become that renowned author, that CEO of a corporation, that outstanding parent, that amazing spouse if you are tormented daily by the what-ifs.

Today's verse is only one of many expressing the importance of giving your anxious thoughts to God and allowing Him to work in all things in your life. He lets us know that we will always have worries because of this fallen world, but we are instructed to live with a hope that He is working all things for our good.

As we read David's psalms, we hear a man who was tormented by the cares of this life. Even though he had so much to worry about as a king, David fell at the feet of a loving and forgiving God who cared for him no matter the struggle.

Why worry? When you cannot change your circumstances, fall into the arms of a loving God. You can do all things through Christ who is your Keeper.

Father, give me wisdom to make the right decisions when troubles come. Allow me to fall into Your arms one more time, and help me turn my worries over to You. In Jesus' name, amen.

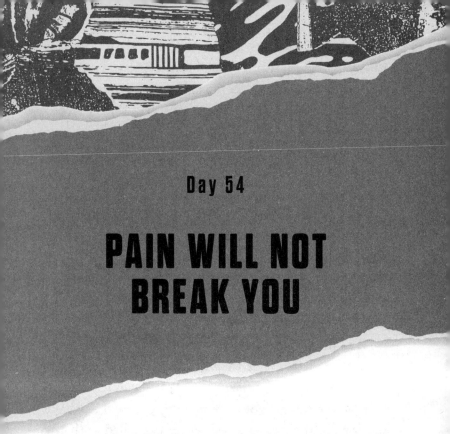

Day 54

PAIN WILL NOT BREAK YOU

I have told you all this so that you may have peace in me. Here on earth you will have many trials and sorrows. But take heart, because I have overcome the world.

—JOHN 16:33

Jesus said that we will have problems in this life, but He doesn't leave us to figure life out on our own.

Instead, He promises peace and reminds us that He has overcome the world. Many run to friends, others to lovers, for solutions to these challenges, yet many times the answers will not come until we accept that He is our bottom line.

When Jesus was assuring His disciples, they were about to face the darkest season of their lives. The Lord would soon be leaving them, not for an extended vacation but because He would be offered up as a sacrifice for the sins of all mankind. This man who had never done wrong would be sold out for thirty pieces of silver by one of His own disciples, then beaten until unrecognizable by Roman soldiers before being nailed to the cross for the sins of all generations.

The disciples scattered and most of them abandoned Him at the cross, but they gathered back together at Pentecost. I am still amazed that Peter, who had denied that he knew Jesus not once but three times before the rooster crowed, was the one who was filled with the Holy Spirit and preached a powerful sermon on the day of Pentecost. If you had told the disciples before that day that Peter would be speaking to thousands about Jesus Christ, they would certainly have disputed your word.

After the crucifixion, the world despised the disciples and many were flogged and even killed for the sake of the gospel, but they stood firm despite this persecution. We can be confident that no matter what pain we bear, Jesus will give us peace. Pain will not break us. We don't have to live in fear, for He has overcome anything that we will ever have to face.

Father, as I face trials in my daily life, give me the assurance that You cause all things to work together for my good. In Jesus' name, amen.

Day 55

PRESS ON

A woman in the crowd had suffered for twelve years with constant bleeding, and she could find no cure. Coming up behind Jesus, she touched the fringe of his robe. Immediately, the bleeding stopped.

—LUKE 8:43–44

I cannot imagine the isolation suffered by this woman in today's Scripture passage. She lived in biblical times when it was considered unclean to have any type of blood loss. After twelve years of living with this pain, suffering, and isolation while spending everything she had on doctors who could not heal her, she determined her only hope was Jesus Christ and ventured out into the public knowing they disdained her. She had not been allowed even in the temple worship because anyone who touched her was also considered unclean. This meant that when she touched Jesus' robe He could have been declared unclean, yet He sensed that a healing anointing had been released. He began asking, "Who touched Me?" There were hundreds pressed against Him, but He knew this touch was different. The woman finally came forward. Jesus told her that her faith had healed her.

Despite the woman's illness, she chose to focus on Jesus Christ. She pressed through the crowd while feeling the hatred of the Jews, who called her unclean. She could have allowed depression and despondency to determine her decisions that day, but she responded through faith and was miraculously set free.

It's easy for us to fall victim to critical voices, but deliverance and healing come when we follow this woman's example by focusing on Jesus. God doesn't cause bad things to happen in our lives, but He can use them for our good and to turn us to Jesus.

Father, when I experience illness and pain, please give me the strength to act in faith and respond to Your voice. Help me lay my suffering and loss at Your feet. In Jesus' name, amen.

Day 56

QUITTING IS NOT AN OPTION

O our God, won't you stop them? We are powerless against this mighty army that is about to attack us. We do not know what to do, but we are looking to you for help.

—2 Chronicles 20:12

When a massive army of three nations attacked King Jehoshaphat and the nation of Judah, the king could have surrendered and immediately given up. Instead, he relied on God and trusted that He would deliver them.

The nation of Judah experienced a miraculous victory that day. Jehoshaphat could have allowed his circumstances to cripple him and his military force. He did not.

This story has brought me solace amid life's challenges when I felt the most alone and did not know what my tomorrow would bring. Even though most of my challenges were the results of my foolish decisions, I eventually turned to God and He always saw me through.

Something happens within us when a crisis arises. Most of us immediately turn to either panic or peace. It took me years of failing at marriage, business, and life in general to look to God for help. However, when I made the decision to trust, God was already there.

Father, as I make today's decisions, help me remember You are the Creator of the entire universe and can change any situation when I walk by faith and not by sight. Today I will change my negatives to positives. In Jesus' name, amen.

Day 57

BUT DID IT KILL YOU?

*If you have raced with men on foot
    and they have worn you out,
    how can you compete with horses?
If you stumble in safe country,
    how will you manage in the thickets by
    the Jordan?*
—JEREMIAH 12:5 NIV

I remember the day I was fired from my job after I was
trying to turn my life around. I had lost my marriage,

home, and business. My boys and I had relocated to my parents' home, and after a year, a local department store had hired me. The day management called me into their office several months later, I was certain I was getting a promotion. Surely I had learned enough to become a department head! So when the store manager told me that he was relieving me of my duties, I was shocked beyond belief.

He told me I was being let go because of time clock fraud. There were certain times I had not clocked out for a break. I was totally humiliated. Everybody had thought I was getting a promotion.

I fell on the couch at home and was content to stay there for the rest of my life. I had a mom, however, who made sure I remembered that I had two boys counting on me. She asked me, "Do you have a disease that will take you to the grave? Are you alone with no one to help you? But did it kill you?" I knew my mom wouldn't allow me to remain unemployed for very long. She knew the rallying call from today's scripture. She gave me an ultimatum: "You can cry now, but then you will get up and find another job."

One hour later, my phone rang but I was too distraught to answer. My mom picked it up, handed it to me, and whispered that life would go on. Estée Lauder at Bloomingdale's was calling and offering me a job that paid more than I had been making. The caller explained that they had been watching my progress but could not hire me because I worked for another company. When they heard I had been fired, they immediately reached out.

I never imagined the turmoil of that morning in the manager's office would result in a time for celebration. Struggles are meant to make us better and more effective for Christ. Our struggles should drive us to our knees in prayer and to the Bible in desperation.

Father, thank You for the struggles that have been good for me. Thank You for the crises that have driven me to my knees to become the best me. In Jesus' name, amen.

RELEASE UNFORGIVENESS

Jesus said, "Father, forgive them, for they don't know what they are doing." And the soldiers gambled for his clothes by throwing dice.

—Luke 23:34

Can you imagine standing in Jesus' shoes as He was sentenced to a death reserved for the worst criminals? Even in this completely unfair situation, He said,

"Father, forgive them, for they don't know what they are doing." That prayer tells us everything we need to know about Jesus Christ. Pilate knew Jesus was innocent but arrested Him to serve the religious leaders' interests. Pilate washed his hands before the crowd to show his innocence in condemning Jesus (Matthew 27:24). The chief priests, elders, and those in the crowd said, "We will take responsibility for his death—we and our children" (v. 25).

However, when Jesus was dying on the cross, He forgave every person who wanted Him to die and even those who participated in His death. He forgave the Jews and even the Romans who nailed Him to the cross. Jesus forgave them, which means they were not held guilty for His death. Remember, He did not die because they willed it to happen. He died because He allowed it to happen.

We can go through life holding resentment and unforgiveness toward those we feel have wronged us; however, to walk in liberty means to be free from anyone who has ever done us wrong. Jesus died on the cross carrying the world's sins, including yours and mine. We each deserve to hang on a cross for our sins, yet He took our place. If Jesus could forgive us, how can we not forgive others?

Father, I know Your mercies are new every morning. You are still the One who forgives my every sin. Give me the desire to forgive as I am forgiven. In Jesus' name, amen.

Never wish them pain; that's not who you are. If they caused you pain, they must have pain inside. Wish them healing.

—RTK

ELEVATION

From that time on, Mephibosheth ate regularly at David's table, like one of the king's own sons.

—2 Samuel 9:11

Elevation means moving from a lower position to a higher one. *Elevation* means repositioning. Mephibosheth, Jonathan's son and King Saul's grandson, was five years old when news came that both his father and grand-father had been killed in battle at Jezreel. When the nurse taking care of him heard the news, she attempted to flee and dropped him. As a result of the fall, he became lame in both feet. He was hidden in Lo Debar, where he remained for fear of being killed. This was a land of no communication, so it seemed he was forgotten. One day he heard a knock on the door that changed his life forever. Mephibosheth relocated to the king's palace.

Mephibosheth had given up completely. In fact, he called himself a dead dog. When King David heard that Jonathan's son was alive, he decreed that Mephibosheth would eat from the king's table all the days of his life. David restored all that Mephibosheth was to have inherited from his father and grandfather.

Your current position is not necessarily an indicator of where God is taking you. God can pick up an orphan like Esther and make her a queen or a shepherd boy like David and make him a king or a stammerer like Moses and make him a leader.

Nothing is impossible with God.

Elevation has a way of repositioning you for your good. Get ready for your own decree to be made in Jesus' name. It's your season of elevation.

Father, as I wait in expectation of my next move, give me the wisdom to choose the right path and allow You to determine my steps. In Jesus' name, amen.

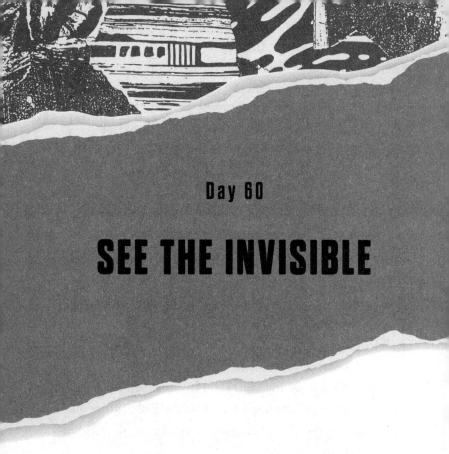

Day 60

SEE THE INVISIBLE

*It was by faith that Moses left the land of
Egypt, not fearing the king's anger. He kept
right on going because he kept his eyes on
the one who is invisible.*

—HEBREWS 11:27

When Pharaoh's daughter discovered a small baby
floating in a basket down the Nile River, she decided
to adopt him. The baby, Moses, was raised in Pharaoh's

palace and had access to the best education of that day. He was guaranteed a life of privilege and prosperity. Yet at forty years of age, Moses' heart was drawn to the Israelite people, his people.

He renounced his place of privilege in Pharaoh's family and chose to identify with God's people when he stepped in and murdered an Egyptian for striking a Hebrew slave (Exodus 2:12). Moses probably assumed that his fellow Israelites would realize that God had sent him to rescue them, but he was wrong (Acts 7:25).

The next day, after he murdered the Egyptian, he visited them again and saw two men of Israel fighting. He tried to be a peacemaker, but the man in the wrong asked Moses who had made him judge and ruler over them. He asked if Moses was going to kill him like he had killed the Egyptian the day before. When Pharaoh discovered that Moses had murdered an Egyptian, he wanted to kill Moses. So Moses fled to the wilderness for forty years (Exodus 2:13–15), then he was called by God to return to Egypt to lead his people out of bondage.

The forty-year-old Moses who had killed the Egyptian was strong, educated, and skilled. He had political power, military knowledge, and was physically gifted. Forty years later, after spending time in the wilderness herding his father-in-law's animals, his dreams of leading anyone out were null and void. He went from, *It makes sense that God would use me* to *Why would God use me?* Then God showed up in a burning bush and called him back to his people.

God knew that Moses was ready to be used and the

timing was right. Eighty-year-old Moses showed up in Egypt with a stutter and a stick, accompanied by Aaron, who spoke for him. The Lord chose Moses because he knew his weakness was a platform for the invisible God's strength. Moses spent the next forty years watching God's glory be revealed to the children of Israel.

Father, I submit myself to You to be used for Your glory. Let Your will manifest itself through my actions. In Jesus' name, amen.

SHOW UP AND SHOW OUT

*When you produce much fruit, you are
my true disciples. This brings great glory
to my Father.*

—JOHN 15:8

Eighty percent of success is showing up or starting the
journey. To get healthy, to lose weight, to begin a fit-
ness plan, you must show up at the gym or walking track.
When I was overweight and depressed, I would lie on

my bed and eat bags of Twizzlers every night. This routine had caused me to put on fifty-five extra pounds. If you knew me during this time, you know I dressed in flowing garments and multiple layers, trying to hide the weight gain.

When my doctor told me that I was overweight, I listened. On my way home from the doctor's, I prayed that God would take the desire for Twizzlers away. I honestly heard Him say, *I can't take the desire away. You must quit buying them. Get them out of your house.* I started to clean all the sugar—cookies, candy, and so forth—out of my cabinets.

Within one month, I had lost thirty pounds and was on a healthy journey. Fifty-five pounds later, I had done the work to detox my body from sugar. A few months after that, I determined it was time to begin running and working out. It has been a daily discipline for me to get to the gym and become the healthy woman God called me to be. Now I not only show up for events but show out because good health has become my friend. My prayer is that I will work with God as He leads me daily on this journey of wellness and health.

It's up to you to take back your life and allow God to be Lord of all you decide to do. You can take the first step to be or do whatever you want by just showing up. For example, if you want to be an author, show up and begin writing your first draft. Someone who makes a plan and follows through with that plan will be more successful than the one sitting at home wishing for change.

Show up and show out.

━━━━━━━━━━

Father, give me direction and understanding as I seek You to become a better me. In Jesus' name, amen.

Day 62

SILENCE THAT NEGATIVE VOICE

I heard a loud voice shouting across the
heavens,
* "It has come at last—*
*   salvation and power*
* and the Kingdom of our God,*
*   and the authority of his Christ.*
* For the accuser of our brothers and sisters*
*   has been thrown down to earth—*
* the one who accuses them*
*   before our God day and night."*

—REVELATION 12:10

Day and night, a spirit called "the accuser of the brethren" brings charges against us before God. Have you wondered why you sometimes feel unworthy, not good enough, ashamed, or condemned? There are spirits attacking you, causing you to question anything positive in your life. The enemy, the devil, "prowls around like a roaring lion, looking for someone to devour" (1 Peter 5:8). He sounds like a roaring lion, so put a muzzle on him. We can stop his constant bantering by the blood of the Lamb and the word of our testimony.

Talk to yourself. Tell yourself how special you are, how you have the mind of Christ and "no weapon formed against you shall prosper" (Isaiah 54:17 NKJV), and the Lord will condemn every tongue that rises against you in judgment. Why would you allow the enemy to break you down and cause you pain when you are called by God to influence the nations?

Start today with a declaration that you are the righteousness of God through Christ Jesus (2 Corinthians 5:21 NIV). Repent for every lie you have believed from the enemy and every action you have taken because of those beliefs. Declare that you are covered by the blood of Jesus today and no weapon formed against you will prosper, in Jesus' name.

Father, thank You for sending Your Son, Jesus, to shed His blood and through His sacrifice set me free. In Jesus' name, amen.

SO MUCH MORE

*So just as sin ruled over all people
and brought them to death, now God's
wonderful grace rules instead, giving us
right standing with God and resulting in
eternal life through Jesus Christ our Lord.*
—Romans 5:21

I n my search for truth during the past few years, I have
learned that sin brings death and we cannot escape
our own sin nature no matter how hard we try. Without
God's intervention, our lives are full of turmoil and trials.

Our lives cannot change just because we want them to change; however, we can allow Jesus Christ to be Lord of every decision, every thought, every action that is processed through our beings each day. Even though our world is full of evil, sin cannot grow past God's capacity to give good to those who deserve His judgment.

We can question the reason God allows so much devastation—from the fall of Adam to the flood to the horrendous death of His Son, Jesus Christ. God knew that eternal life would not come from the first man, Adam. He knew that even His own people, the children of Israel, would sin and need a Savior. God heard the cries of the Israelites in Egypt, and He knew they would fail Him miserably even though He sent Moses to bring them out. He knew that sin would rule over His people and death would be the end, so He sent grace.

God sent His only Son to stand in our place and to take our sins in His body on the cross so that we could be made righteous. At creation God had a plan. Grace was planned, as was Jesus Christ's crucifixion and resurrection. As sin reigned in death, grace would reign through righteousness eternally. It is by faith and by faith alone that we receive the grace of justification and obtain eternal life.

Father, I repent to You today for not only my sins but the sins of the fathers through generations past. I accept the grace that is sufficient for my sins and stand on Your promises. In Jesus' name, amen.

SPEAK YOUR FAITH

It is written: "I believed; therefore I have spoken." Since we have that same spirit of faith, we also believe and therefore speak.
—2 CORINTHIANS 4:13 NIV

You and I are made in God's image. God spoke the universe into existence. The creative act of speaking matter into existence out of nothing sets Him apart as God. Because God spoke everything into existence, His creation reveals His glory. Jesus spoke to the storm, and it subsided. He then spoke to the demons, and they had to flee. Jesus spoke to the sick, and they were healed. It was all about the spoken word. He was giving us, His church, the example of being able to speak our faith and see miracles happen. If we find ourselves facing any type of dangerous situation or sickness, Jesus taught us to declare His Word.

God loves what He created, and we are His creation. There is an intimate connection between God and that which He spoke into being. We are created in His image and have that power to speak life into dead situations.

To be able to speak our faith means we must believe that God is orchestrating each step of our lives. As believers we have the same spirit, power, and potential as Jesus Christ through His Holy Spirit. The faith of David, Daniel, Peter, and Paul is the same faith that we have as believers today.

Identify several verses to memorize and have available to quote and "speak your faith." Jude verse 20 tells us to build each other up in our faith by praying in the Holy Spirit. Matthew 21:21 says that with faith and no doubt, you can tell a mountain, "May you be lifted up and thrown into the sea." And it will be done.

You shall see things shift in your life when you walk in faith. For faith to operate it must be released through spoken words, according to Jesus. What you speak is evidence of your faith.

Father, as I face challenges in my daily walk, give me the power and insight to speak life and believe that things will change. In Jesus' name, amen.

TALK TO YOURSELF

The tongue can bring death or life;
those who love to talk will reap the
consequences.

—Proverbs 18:21

Our speech can reap both positive and negative results.
I live in a positive world today because I continually make declarations over my circumstances. My day
is filled with positive affirmations over my life. If you

had asked me when I was a child what my future would resemble, I would never have imagined a life filled with godliness, joy, peace, and tranquility. I struggled with a learning disability beginning in the first grade and could see no positive outcome. I never imagined a social media world filled with millions of followers who cared what I had to say. Yet here I am daily speaking life through small thumbnails on numerous social media platforms.

I have become an ambassador for Christ who is loving people back to life. In fact, I live to love those who feel unlovable. I awake daily seeking the wisdom of God as I speak life into thousands who are online with me. I choose my words carefully because they have the power to bring life. Having the courage to speak the truth while weeding out harsh criticisms and unkind thoughts allows you to bring life to those you love. Be conscientious as you speak because your words help determine your future and give life or death to those who hear them.

Father, as I respond to You today, help me become the carrier of Your presence. Let me speak life into every situation and over everyone I encounter. I give You authority to rule and reign in each day of my life. In Jesus' name, amen.

Day 66

TRIUMPH OVER IT

In that coming day
no weapon turned against you will
succeed.
You will silence every voice
raised up to accuse you.
These benefits are enjoyed by the servants
of the LORD;
their vindication will come from me.
I, the LORD, *have spoken!*
— ISAIAH 54:17

The prophet Isaiah delivered a message from God about the restoration of Jerusalem after its destruction by the Babylonians. God promised the people they would be able to return to their land and live there without fear of further devastation. God promised that no enemy would come against them and succeed. Of course, enemies would come against them, but those enemies could not succeed because God was on their side. I continually quote this verse because I apply His promises whenever I am battling the enemy. The primary theme God wants to communicate in this passage is that He is our salvation, so whom should we fear?

Even when bad things happen, and they do, we can trust and not be afraid. Even when a crisis strikes our nation, sickness spreads quickly throughout the world, or wars and rumors of wars are causing devastation in many countries, we know that the time is not over because we haven't won yet. If you're still breathing, God is still working for you.

The weapons we fight with are not the weapons of this world. Even when the enemy hits us with spiritual strongholds of confusion, depression, anger, doubt, temptation, and anxiety, the Lord has given us His Word as our sword and faith as our shield. He will never leave us nor forsake us. His promise to us is that no weapon turned against us shall succeed, and we will silence every voice raised up in accusation. At the end of the day, God wins and His people prosper.

We will win in the end! Take it to the bank and invest it!

Father, as I face temptations and trials, give me the insight to lift up my eyes and focus on You rather than my circumstances. In Jesus' name, amen.

Day 67

TURN IT AROUND

Then I will purify the speech of all people,
so that everyone can worship the
LORD together.
—ZEPHANIAH 3:9

We all have faced situations that look as though
they'll never change. It's easy to get discouraged. In

Zephaniah 3:9 the writer prophesies that the speech of the entire nation will be made pure, pointing to the day when there will no longer be sin. As I reflect on my life and the many decisions that created the Kimberly Jones you know, I realize that God saw something in me when I was totally broken and unsure how to keep going. He loves each of us despite our decisions and failures. God knew that on this day you would be reaching for my ideas on how to turn your brokenness into His planned stability. I had no idea how to change the life I had chosen; however, I knew God was my source.

To allow God to create in you a clean heart and pure mind is to determine that you will no longer be the one in control of your destiny. It's so easy to do life the way you plan—until it doesn't work. Then you must address your issues and acknowledge that you alone cannot change your life. You must surrender what you can't control and allow the Creator of this universe to do what He does best. If God can order our steps and work things out for our good, why do we question His directions in our personal lives?

God spoke to Abram (later called Abraham) and told him to take his wife and leave his family to go to the land God would show Him (Genesis 12). God asked Abram to respond in obedience to something that seemed to have no reason and no logic, yet Abram obeyed. To do the will of the Father may not make sense or seem realistic, but when God says move you just move. For your conditions to change, act on faith not fear, and watch God turn your life around.

Father, as I make the decision today to respond to Your call, give me the understanding of faith that assists me in choosing life instead of death. In Jesus' name, amen.

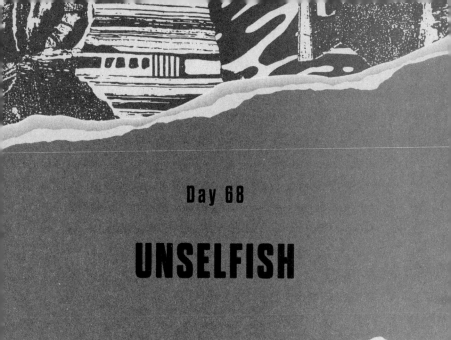

Day 68

UNSELFISH

*Jesus replied, "'You must love the LORD
your God with all your heart, all your soul,
and all your mind.' This is the first and
greatest commandment. A second is equally
important: 'Love your neighbor as yourself.'"*
—MATTHEW 22:37–39

We live in a world that doesn't help us pursue self-lessness. In fact, it encourages selfishness and self-idolization. We pose for selfies, edit our photos, and self-promote the best parts of our lives. We post selfies to get likes while spending hours reading the comments and refreshing notifications. Our social media posts shout, "Look at me. Look at what I'm doing! Look at what I've accomplished!" The more we think of ourselves, the less we think of others. We're continually on a fast track of weight loss or muscle gain while thinking less and less of others' needs. We rarely ignore our needs, yet Jesus told us to think of our neighbors with the same affection we think of ourselves. We must love them, seek out their needs, and care for them.

Paul told us to be unselfish, to not try to impress others, and to be humble, thinking of others as better than ourselves. He said to not only look out for our own interest but to take an interest in others (Philippians 2:3–4). To walk out Paul's mandate in our present lives means we must turn the selfie lens away from our faces, our needs, and our wants, and turn our attention toward others and toward Christ.

When we're no longer fixated on me, me, me, we begin using our resources for others and seeing people who could use a hand when we have one available. The "love your neighbor as yourself" instruction means we must love ourselves as people God created so we can love those He has called into our lives.

Father, give me insight into love that will reach out to my neighbors daily. Help me love me so I can love those You have brought into my life. In Jesus' name, amen.

Day 69

WELCOME CHANGE

Don't copy the behavior and customs of this world, but let God transform you into a new person by changing the way you think. Then you will learn to know God's will for you, which is good and pleasing and perfect.

—ROMANS 12:2

I called my spiritual sister and Realtor to let her know that I was ready to sell my home and move downtown to the high-rise I had always envisioned living in. I can't explain why that day was the day for change, but it was as though I had been planning this move for ages. She explained that my house would sell in a day, so I needed to know where I was moving. I set a date to spy out condos that could be my future home.

I knew the first condo I walked into was mine. I wanted to look out over the amazing city that God had brought our family to when I was a six-year-old little girl. When they were evangelizing, my dad and mom would ride through this beautiful city during the night to look at the high-rises lit up like Christmas. When they received the news that some families wanted to start a new church in a suburb of Atlanta, my parents knew God wanted them in this city they loved.

Now I begin my busy days doing my Father's will, looking out over this bustling, thriving city from a penthouse view. My parents would never have imagined that not only would I be living in the middle of the energy of Atlanta, but also my brother and his family and even my mom now have their own places downtown. Mom often says that my dad, who passed several years ago, would love where she is living.

Our beautiful life could not have happened if my family and I were not welcoming to change. We have always been a ministry family and available for whatever God wanted us to do next. The first four years of my life were spent in an RV, traveling from church to church for revivals. Back then, revivals lasted from four to six weeks, so we took up residence and made each town our home.

It's easy for me to welcome change because change has been good to me.

Do your part and allow change to do you good.

———

Father, I welcome change in this season. Help me become the me that You want me to be as I cut off the old and welcome the new. In Jesus' name, amen.

God is going to send you places you will feel you aren't qualified to go. Trust God and go. He knows you better than you know you.

—RTK

WHAT'S HOLDING YOU BACK?

There was a man named Nicodemus, a Jewish religious leader who was a Pharisee. After dark one evening, he came to speak with Jesus. "Rabbi," he said, "we all know that God has sent you to teach us. Your miraculous signs are evidence that God is with you."

Jesus replied, "I tell you the truth, unless you are born again, you cannot see the Kingdom of God."

—JOHN 3:1–3

icodemus visited Jesus in the night. Isn't that a strange time to be knocking on someone's door? This man was a respected teacher in Israel and was set apart with about six thousand other Pharisees, yet he wanted to hear what Jesus had to say. Nicodemus was hungry for more of the teachings of Jesus, but he knew he would be ostracized if people had any idea of his desires. They would wonder why in the world this teacher, a member of the respected Sanhedrin Court, would risk his reputation to spend time with this "renegade," as Jesus was known by the Pharisees. Nicodemus is a great example of someone who was so hungry for more truth that he risked it all to satisfy his desire.

Being raised in a pastor's home, I wonder how I could have spent every Sunday sitting in the front pew of our church and still walked away at eighteen because I allowed the cares of this world, instead of Jesus, to lead me. I wonder how much more I could have accomplished if I had understood the love of Jesus when I was younger.

Ask yourself, *What's holding me back? What keeps me from accomplishing those dreams that have been a constant since I was a child?*

We know that Nicodemus went to Jesus at night because he was afraid of being seen. He was seeking safety in the darkness. Nicodemus quickly learned that there is nothing safe about knowing Jesus, but there is good. It's not about being safe. It's about finding that purpose for which you were created. It's doing the will of the Father and allowing Him to be Lord of every situation in your life. Don't allow fear to hold you back. Just move!

Father, give me the fortitude to stand up and do what is right. As I make decisions today, I will declare that Jesus is Lord to the glory of the Father. In Jesus' name, amen.

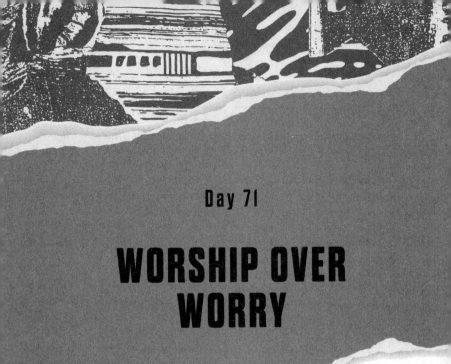

Day 71

WORSHIP OVER WORRY

For the weapons of our warfare are not carnal but mighty in God for pulling down strongholds, casting down arguments and every high thing that exalts itself against the knowledge of God, bringing every thought into captivity to the obedience of Christ.

—2 CORINTHIANS 10:4–5 NKJV

Christianity isn't for wimps. It takes courageous men and women to serve Jesus Christ. People all over the world are being persecuted for Christ's sake. Even though we live in a nation that isn't suffering violent oppression for our faith, we see our nation becoming more secularized daily. When you are faced with opposition, it's natural to be afraid. So how do you deal with fear of loss or persecution or abandonment? You may be worried about a wayward child, divorce, sickness, or financial difficulties, but Paul gave us instructions for winning the war over worry. He said to go from worry to worship by casting down anything that exalts itself against the knowledge of God. The Bible says there is no fear in love and perfect love casts out all fear (1 John 4:18).

You have two choices when you feel pressured to give in to feelings of worry and negativity. You can allow the what-ifs to steal your peace and rob you of your joy, or you can determine that God is in control and worship Him. If you're a Christian, you have hope in a Savior who cares for you. Worry doesn't have to be a constant struggle if we allow the peace of Jesus Christ to rule in our hearts. Worry doesn't leave much room for praise or worship, so it's important to enter into His presence with thanksgiving. When worship enters, worry flees.

Don't waste another day worrying about things you cannot change. Determine what is your responsibility and what is not, and don't try to take on anything that is God's responsibility. Give yourself and your worries to God, then trust Him to do what you cannot do. Open yourself up to worship and begin enjoying His abundant life.

———

Father, I give up anything in my life that makes me feel desperate and unable to cope. I will allow You to be Lord of every area of my life. In Jesus' name, amen.

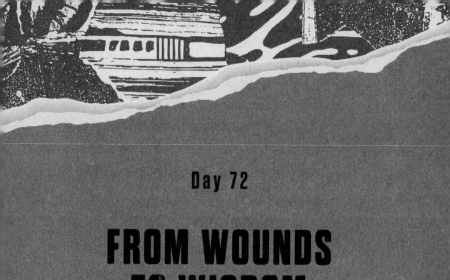

FROM WOUNDS TO WISDOM

We know that God causes everything to work together for the good of those who love God and are called according to his purpose for them.

—Romans 8:28

We're all broken people born into a world full of sin. Sometimes we hurt each other intentionally and other times unintentionally. We're not perfect and life's not fair, so it's up to each of us to learn to deal with failure and mistakes with forgiveness and then to move on.

Adam and Eve, the first man and woman created by God, were given the responsibility to care for the garden of Eden. They could eat from any tree except the Tree of Knowledge of Good and Evil. When they allowed the serpent to tempt them into eating of the fruit of that tree, they set up each of us—for generations to come—to experience the pain of failure.

Have you wondered—as I have—how this couple, born into a perfect place and having daily communion with the Creator of the universe, would choose to act exactly opposite of what He had instructed? They had dominion over everything—including the fish, the birds, and every living thing that moved on the earth at that time (Genesis 1:28)—except the one little tree in the middle of the garden. We don't know how many trees were there—it could have been thousands. They were only instructed to leave that *one* tree alone.

Satan targeted Eve, who then persuaded Adam to take a bite of the fruit. Immediately they knew they had committed sin. As soon as the shame, guilt, and condemnation set in, they lost their childlike innocence and purity. They were banished from the garden and God pronounced a curse on the serpent and the earth. Poverty and lack entered the world when they ate of the forbidden fruit.

Wisdom is what the serpent offered Adam and Eve. They had no idea their disobedience would open up a new world of pain and misunderstandings. Does this sound familiar? When we fail to listen to God's voice, we, too, experience pain and loss. Determine that you will allow the Lord Jesus to rule and reign in your life and guide all your decisions.

———

Father, turn my wounds into wisdom as I determine to follow You in my daily life. In Jesus' name, amen.

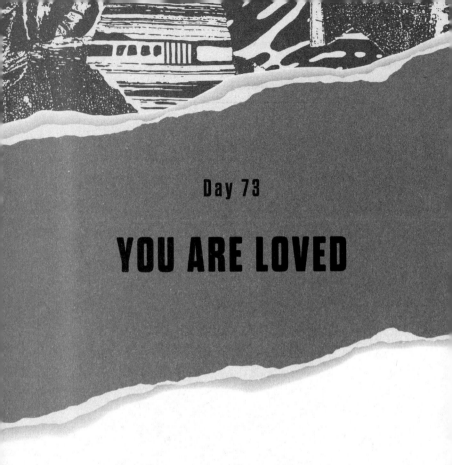

YOU ARE LOVED

For this is how God loved the world: He gave his one and only Son, so that everyone who believes in him will not perish but have eternal life.

—JOHN 3:16

One of the first Bible verses I remember reading was the "love verse." No matter how far I journeyed from the love of those who surrounded me daily, I could never quite hide from the fact that, no matter my condition, God loved me. I may not have spoken to Him daily, but when I needed Him, I knew who to call. I now realize I took advantage of God's love so many times, but He never took advantage of me. I remember times when I knew my marriage was truly over, even while I was attempting to stand firm in the truth that God loved marriage and would assist me in making things right. My confidence was not because I was such a good person or had been loyal to the faith or even to the church; I stood on His promise that if He loved me enough to give His Son in my place, then He wanted my marriage to work. I was so caught up in thinking that everything revolved around my happiness, my success.

The day I finally realized that God was the Creator of the entire universe and not just me, my life was changed. I cried out for Him to please bring my husband back to me. In the stillness of my room, I heard Him say, "You never asked Me if he was the one." Even though God did not bless the mess of a marriage that I had selfishly entered, I began a journey to find the purpose that God had created me for when He knitted me in the darkness of my mother's womb. I had never come face-to-face with the reality that God made me specifically for a certain time and place. That He had a call, a purpose for me, and it was bigger than I could imagine. That He loved me so much that He gave His only Son to die in my place so I could have eternal life.

I'm telling you that He loves you more than you can

imagine. Give Him the place He deserves in your heart and allow Him to change your life.

———

Father, understanding Your love for me changed my love for You. I give You that place in my heart that You deserve. Make me what You desire me to be. In Jesus' name, amen.

Day 74

YOU MATTER

See, I have written your name on the palms of my hands.
—Isaiah 49:16

W e each have a desire to be loved and appreciated, to build relationships and feel significant. We all want to believe that if we die, someone will care. We spend time contemplating who cares enough to want to spend time with us. No matter how much we're worth, how many miles we've traveled, how many relationships we have built, or how popular we have become, none of it matters unless we first build a relationship with Jesus Christ. Nothing in this life lasts unless we have the foundation of love found in Jesus.

One day, as we stand before God, we will see the nail scars in His hands where He took on suffering and pain so that we could have everlasting life. If you base your life's worth on the opinions of others, you will collapse under the pressure of criticism, rejection, and judgment that is a natural part of living in a fallen world.

When you build your self-worth on the knowledge that you were distinctly created by God, who loves you unconditionally, who gave His life on the cross for you, and who has gone to prepare a place for you, you will be able to stand. When you know how much you're worth to God, you will be able to affirm the worth of those in your life.

Jesus thought you were worth dying for, so now live in such a way that you bring glory to His name.

Father, thank You for sending Your Son to die for me so that I can live for You. Give me insight into the sacrifices You made for me so that I can be a living example of You. In Jesus' name, amen.

Day 75

YOUR PURPOSE IS HIDDEN IN YOUR PAIN

*Jesus told him, "Stand up, pick up your
mat, and walk!"*

—John 5:8

Physical pain is the body's alert system that something is wrong, something needs to be dealt with. It is also true that until you experience emotional or spiritual pain and realize you are broken emotionally or spiritually, you cannot begin the journey of healing. Your purpose is hidden in your pain. If everything works for your good, as Scripture says, then you must understand your pain does as well. To become unstuck, you must determine what to do *in* your pain and what to do *with* your pain. Honestly, I would never have faced the reality that I had sabotaged my business, my marriage, and my family until I came face-to-face with my pain.

You can wallow in your pain or flip the script and determine that tomorrow will be different. No one can make you get up until you decide you don't want to stay broken. Remember the man at the pool of Bethesda who had been broken for thirty-eight years (John 5)? He had to obey Jesus' command to get up. Jesus told him to take up his bed and walk. He had to get rid of the props that had been with him for so long. If he removed his mat, he would not be able to return to it if he had a bad day. It was his choice to decide to move. It was his opportunity to gain freedom from pain, and he made the choice to obey and move even though he did not fully understand.

You can make the same choice today. Just do it. Just get up and start moving and watch God do what He does best.

Father, as I get up and leave my pain today, give me the strength to keep moving forward. In Jesus' name, amen.

A WORK IN PROGRESS

You know what I am going to say
  even before I say it, LORD.
You go before me and follow me.
  You place your hand of blessing on my
    head.
Such knowledge is too wonderful for me,
  too great for me to understand!

—PSALM 139:4–6

Have you wondered what your life would look like if things were different? If you had earned a different degree or joined a different company? If you had married your high school sweetheart or bought the house that you wanted in the beginning? Most people don't live as if they are works in progress. They don't realize they are projects created by God that are not yet finished.

Just because you made a mistake, dropped out of school, or left a certain job does not mean your life is over. You have tomorrow to change things.

What comes out of our mouths is the result of the words we form in our minds. God knows our thoughts. He searches out the pathway ahead and understands our failures and our successes. God knows that we are each a work in progress. We fall and get back up, fall again and one more time get up because God is in charge. He is the Potter, and we are the clay.

With God, there is always hope, clarity, peace, protection, and promise. He will mold us into His likeness as long as we remain under His care. I wake up each morning with an assurance that God has already structured my day. It's up to me to walk in the steps He has ordered.

Give Him the opportunity to be God and decide today will be your best day yet.

Father, as I live my life, help me get up one more time than I fall down. Give me grace to forgive myself when I fall and know that I remain in Your care. In Jesus' name, amen.

Day 77

FREEDOM TO SOAR

Those who trust in the LORD will find
  new strength.
  They will soar high on wings like eagles.
They will run and not grow weary.
They will walk and not faint.
  —ISAIAH 40:31

Perhaps you've heard this inspirational fable about an eagle. According to the legend, at around forty years old the eagle must make the difficult decision to die or go through a painful rebirth.

In its old age, unable to use his talons for hunting or wings for flying, the eagle will fly to the top of a mountain to nest for about 150 days. In the nest he'll knock his beak against a rock until it falls off. Once a new beak grows in, he'll use it to pull out his talons. Waiting for the new talons to grow, he'll begin plucking out his feathers. Five months later, the "reborn" eagle takes flight and can live another thirty years. This could never have happened if he had not allowed the process to take place. What an amazing journey!

Wouldn't it be wonderful if we could be totally reborn—like the eagle in the fable—by emptying all the baggage we have managed to collect and be totally transformed? I have good news! When we accept Jesus as Lord of our lives, including our thoughts and decisions, we can go through a total transformation and become reborn, releasing all the pent-up baggage we have collected.

This story of the magnificent eagle may be just a legend, but we can share that type of amazing recovery as we determine we only want to process life through the forgiveness of Jesus Christ, who went to the cross and took our sins in His body so we could live a righteous life.

Father, I release all the pain and anguish that life has dealt me and receive Your righteousness so I can become whole in You. In Jesus' name, amen.

Day 78

ONE RIGHT DECISION

Then Joshua secretly sent out two spies
from the Israelite camp at Acacia Grove.
He instructed them, "Scout out the land on
the other side of the Jordan River, especially
around Jericho." So, the two men set out
and came to the house of a prostitute
named Rahab and stayed there that night.

—Joshua 2:1

Before the Israelites crossed the Jordan River, Joshua sent two men to scout out the land. Arriving in Jericho, they came to spend the night at the prostitute Rahab's house. She knew the Lord had already given them the land, so she negotiated a deal with the two spies. She would keep them safe if they would protect her family.

When the king of Jericho heard that Israelites were in the city spying out the land, he ordered Rahab to bring out the men who had stayed at her house. Rahab replied that the men had already left; however, she had hidden them on the roof beneath bundles of flax.

Rahab was known as a prostitute, yet after the invasion, her family was not only saved but she began to nurture hope. Hope for change, hope for a different life, hope for forgiveness for all she had done. Her hope was based on what she had learned about the Israelites' God, who was unlike any gods she had experienced.

In protecting the two spies, Rahab received a new life. She became part of the community who had saved her and her family. She left a life of shame to become a wife and mother. Most amazing, Rahab, the prostitute, would become the great-great-grandmother of David, the psalmist. Expectation can be birthed from this story for all who feel as if their hopeless lives will never change.

God is a God of mercy and forgiveness. It takes only one decision at the right time and the right place to see change for your present and your future.

Father, give me the wisdom to know when to change and the fortitude to make change when it's my time. In Jesus' name, amen.

FROM SCARS TO STARS

They told him, "We have seen the Lord!"
But he replied, "I won't believe it unless I
see the nail wounds in his hands, put my
fingers into them, and place my hand into
the wound in his side."
—JOHN 20:25

After Jesus had resurrected from the dead, He appeared before His disciples, but they did not recognize Him.

It was only when He showed them His scars that they knew He was Jesus. Thomas, one of the twelve disciples, had not been there when Jesus appeared before them, so when they excitedly exclaimed that they had seen Jesus, Thomas doubted. He told them he would not believe Jesus was back unless he saw Jesus' scars in His hands and put his own finger in Jesus' side.

One week later, Jesus appeared again before the men and Thomas was with them. Jesus told Thomas to touch His scars and put his finger in His side. He said, "Don't be faithless anymore."

Thomas shouted, "My Lord and my God!"

Jesus said that he, Thomas, believed because he had seen, but those who believed without seeing are truly blessed.

I still have a small scar on my cheek that was the result of a fall at our church daycare when I was three years old. My mom was reading a book for the kids before naptime. I was running across the room to sit with the group when I slid on a tiny toy that had been left on the floor. My cheek met the corner of a chair and immediately blood poured from my face. The wound required stitches.

My mom was devastated that I would have a scar for the rest of my life. Now I look at my face and don't even notice the scar because it has become a familiar part of me. Even though we have scars, internally and externally, they are all part of the process. Even though Jesus was resurrected, He still carried the scars. I like to think that

His scars turned into stars—proof that He is who He said
He is.

━━━━━━━━━━

*Father, help me to believe and not have doubt, and help me
turn my scars into stars. In Jesus' name, amen.*

Day 80

GET READY TO RISE

> The godly may trip seven times, but they
> will get up again.
> But one disaster is enough to
> overthrow the wicked.
>
> —Proverbs 24:16

It makes a difference how you are living when you fall. Compare the man who is seeking to live righteously with the wicked man who has no concept of righteousness.

The righteous man may fall but will get up one more time than he falls down. He will take his troubles to the Lord and ask for forgiveness one more time. A wicked man will not seek forgiveness because he doesn't feel he is in the wrong.

Sometimes it's difficult to face truth and then walk in repentance when your Adam-nature wants to cover up your sin. When someone falls, it's easy for others to judge that he is living in sin without giving him a chance to repent.

I spent years living with guilt because I just could not become all that I thought I was supposed to be for my church. At thirty-eight years old, I finally began forgiving those who had judged me so harshly, those who had pressed me to be perfect, and those who were living hypocritically. I realized that it was strictly by God's grace that I could live in peace and know that He would forgive me when I fell.

Yes, I would fall, but I made up my mind to get up one more time—just like today's scripture says—and allow God to create in me a clean heart. I finally understand what it means to be godly. It's not about appearance or how hard you work for the church. It's about loving God first and then your neighbor as yourself.

Father, thank You for forgiving me each time I fall and giving me the strength to rise again. Despite my failures, I will walk out the plans You have for me. In Jesus' name, amen.

Day 81

GROW THROUGH IT

*My brethren, count it all joy when you fall
into various trials.*

—James 1:2 NKJV

A s Jesus called the twelve disciples to become His followers, He knew they were an unlikely bunch who were not prepared for the trials ahead. Jesus knew He would go to the cross eventually, so He selected a group to mentor who would carry on the gospel of the kingdom after He was resurrected and no longer physically on earth. As Jesus and His disciples walked together for three and a half years, God's purpose was that this group of men would grow and become more and more like Jesus Christ.

God's perspective is not the same as ours. He sees the purpose and outcome of each trial we face. He knew these men would be persecuted and even killed for the sake of the gospel. He knew their futures when they only had the perspective of their present.

These disciples walked with Jesus, and they felt sure He could and would protect them. They saw Him raise the dead, heal the blind, and cast out demons. Surely He could do anything. They had no idea that He would be taken from them, persecuted, and then crucified.

James wrote that we should count it joy when we are faced with trials. He said, "When you fall into trials." The word *fall* means to do so unexpectedly. Trials are not planned. We cannot anticipate all the problems we will face. If we could, we would probably run the other way and not receive their benefits.

Don't be surprised by your trials. They are coming. You can face them and become a much better person because of them. Grow through it!

Father, as trials come my way, give me the strength to not only become a victor in my daily life but also to grow from the experience. In Jesus' name, amen.

Hold on! God is going to give you back twofold for every tear you shed and every regret that comes to mind. He is going to heal your wounded heart.

—RTK

Day 82

HAVE FAITH

Give your entire attention to what God is doing right now, and don't get worked up about what may or may not happen tomorrow. God will help you deal with whatever hard things come up when the time comes.

—MATTHEW 6:34 MSG

We live in a world full of uncertainties. Recently my mother was doing her normal daily exercises and completed ten push-ups. About two hours later, she felt a persistent, severe pain in her chest. After about five more hours, she became nauseated and threw up. She knew she needed to be checked for serious complications. Her symptoms indicated she might be suffering a heart attack, so after several hours at the hospital, the doctors and nurses determined she would spend the night there for more testing.

Throughout the next day, the medical staff continually watched her. They determined she needed to spend another night in the hospital for even more tests. My mom is a very busy lady who constantly works on her computer; however, she had not brought her computer to the hospital. She insisted there was no need to bring her computer to her; she would just be a good patient and wait for the results.

Three days later, after finally figuring out the chest pains had probably been from a pulled muscle, my mom was ready to leave, but the doctors identified a heart condition unrelated to the chest pains that would never have been noticed if she had not been in the hospital.

We watched Mom—who had recently lost her husband to dementia and had just moved to a condo after selling our family home—trust the Lord with her health; our family cherished Matthew 6:34 even more.

When faith is a constant, life's challenges will be dealt with accordingly. Why worry about the uncertainties when you cannot change many of them anyway? When you realize that God will take care of you, you can sleep soundly at night knowing He is there.

Father, whether I am awake or asleep, You already know my every need, and You want to care for me. Give me the faith to see life through. In Jesus' name, amen.

Day 83

HEALING FROM YOUR FEELINGS

The LORD is close to the brokenhearted;
he rescues those whose spirits are
crushed.

—PSALM 34:18

Every day I receive emails and texts from people who are hurting from previous relationships. I am trusted with the raw truth of hurting families, marriages gone awry, and even young people who blame parents for their failures. I ask God why I am entrusted with the emotional progress of people seeking a better life.

I often ask these people how they are coping with all the pain they carry. I get answers such as, "I just shove it to the back and move forward." But they aren't moving forward. They are stuck in their feelings because they need healing. I explain that Jesus did not come to merely heal our hearts but also to use those painful experiences to teach us more about Him. When we shove our feelings into a drawer, we aren't really living. We are simply existing, carrying baggage full of painful memories.

Many psalms were written about the struggles of daily life. In one psalm David may be crying out to God for deliverance from his enemies, and in the next psalm he will be thanking God for his deliverance. The psalmist pours out his pain as God pours His truth into him.

Our willingness to forgive will bring us the same kind of solace that David wrote about. If we refuse to forgive others, our own emotional healing is short-circuited. Only through forgiving others can we begin to heal from turmoil, grief, pain, rejection, and depression.

We must deal with our past to move forward into our future with confidence that God has it already prepared.

Father, give me direction in finding solace for the pain that I have carried and freedom to choose Your way. In Jesus' name, amen.

IF YOU ONLY KNEW

*Jesus replied, "If you only knew the gift
God has for you and who you are speaking
to, you would ask me, and I would give
you living water."*

—JOHN 4:10

Jesus was speaking to a shunned Samaritan woman who met Him when she went to draw water at the well in the middle of the day. Unlike the women of the town who gathered in the cool of the evening, this woman was coming to draw her water alone because she was an outcast. She was a divorcee, living with a man who was not her husband, and she was a favorite topic of many conversations. When she arrived at the well, Jesus was waiting for her. Although this woman always looked for love in the wrong places and suffered tremendously from shame and guilt, Jesus knew there was purpose for her life. He was ready to help her change.

This woman realized that Jesus was unlike anyone she had ever met. This Jewish man was conversing with her, a Samaritan, even though the Jews saw the Samaritans as inferior. Also, no respectable Jewish teacher would ever be seen alone in public with a woman who wasn't his wife or a close relative. Even her own people thought she was scandalous, yet this man, Jesus, took time to tell her that He did not judge her for her past. He was seeing her future.

Jesus talked about giving her living water—something that would satisfy her thirst forever. This woman was so radically changed because of her divine appointment with Jesus Christ that she ran into the city to tell everyone that they must come meet the man who knew everything she had ever done (John 4:28–29).

Father, while I go about my day, give me the insight to see the plans You have laid out for me as I influence those I meet. In Jesus' name, amen.

IF YOU AIN'T DEAD, GOD AIN'T DONE

*The temptations in your life are no different
from what others experience. And God is
faithful. He will not allow the temptation
to be more than you can stand. When you
are tempted, he will show you a way out so
that you can endure.*

—1 CORINTHIANS 10:13

Most of us have been told that God won't put more on us than we can bear or God won't give us more trials than we can handle. Today's verse explains that our temptations are no different from those that others experience. He promises to show us a way out of each temptation. Paul and his companions were burdened beyond their strength and expected to die. As a result of their crisis, they testified that they stopped relying on their own strength and learned to rely on God, who raises the dead (2 Corinthians 1:8–11).

Paul explained that because he was the most learned of the apostles, he could easily have been caught up in pride of who he was and what he had accomplished. He was given a thorn in the flesh to keep him grounded, which he described as a messenger of Satan who harassed him. Three times he pleaded for God to take the thorn in his side away, but God told him, "My grace is sufficient for you, for my power is made perfect in weakness" (2 Corinthians 12:7–10 NIV).

God doesn't take our temptations away, but He does give us the grace we need for each situation. Paul said that when he wasn't able in his own might to face his suffering, he found power in God's grace to provide what he needed.

No matter how bad your situation is, accept that God will never leave you, never forsake you, and will always give you the grace to stand. If you ain't dead, God ain't done with you.

Father, thank You for the grace of Jesus Christ who covers and protects me in any challenging crisis. In Jesus' name, amen.

I decree and declare to you that God is delivering you from pain to purpose, from stagnation to success, from hurt to health, and from wounds to wisdom.

—RTK

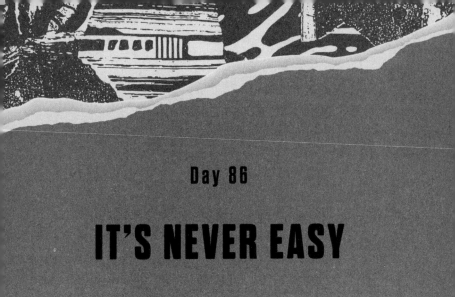

IT'S NEVER EASY

The king said, "Let's get the facts straight.
Both of you claim the living child is yours,
and each says that the dead one belongs to
the other. All right, bring me a sword." So a
sword was brought to the king.

—1 KINGS 3:23–24

There were two mothers living in the same house who
approached King Solomon for advice. Each mother
had a baby son; however, one of the babies had been

smothered during the night. Each mother claimed the living baby was her child. Solomon could not tell from their words which woman was telling the truth, so he called for a sword as he declared his judgment. The living baby would be cut in two, and each woman would receive half.

One mother did not contest the ruling, while the second mother begged Solomon not to kill the baby and give the baby to the other woman. Solomon, known for his wisdom, declared the second woman to be the true mother. Did Solomon really intend to cut the baby in half?

When my phone rang in the early morning hours and I received word that my son had been arrested for driving under the influence, I had no idea what my next move would be. If you had told me that he was going to spend the night in jail, I would have told you that my son would never spend the night in such a place. And yet it was the right thing to make the decision not to immediately bail him out. In fact, he was not released until the next day, late afternoon. I was heartbroken my son was locked up, but I can tell you now that it changed his life.

Life is not easy. But with God's help, we can make wise decisions.

Father, thank You that, despite our decisions, You always come through for us. You give us the strength to do whatever is needed when we look to You. In Jesus' name, amen.

MOUNTAINS TO MOLEHILLS

*Nothing, not even a mighty mountain,
will stand in Zerubbabel's way; it will
become a level plain before him! And
when Zerubbabel sets the final stone of
the Temple in place, the people will shout:
"May God bless it! May God bless it!"*

—ZECHARIAH 4:7

After the Jewish people experienced exile in Babylon, King Cyrus of Persia allowed fifty thousand Jews to return and rebuild the temple under Zerubbabel, governor of Jerusalem. During this time God gave Zechariah, a prophet and priest of Israel, visions concerning the Jews and the building of the temple. In one of those visions God spoke, "'Not by might nor by power, but by my Spirit,' says the LORD Almighty" (Zechariah 4:6 NIV).

As construction began on the temple, hindrances from every side delayed it. In fact, construction was finally halted for a while because of the opposition. The Samaritans who came against the Israelites as they were building the temple had become like a mountain of human obstacles, frustrating them and preventing them from doing what God had commanded.

You may relate to this situation as you face obstacles in your own life. You may feel that God has told you to do something but the enemy has thrown up a mountain in your path. The problem is your perspective.

God told Zechariah that nothing, not even a mighty mountain, would stand in his way. Your mountain is only a molehill to God. Instead of focusing on your problems, remember our God is an awesome God. He would never tell you to do something if He did not know you were capable of finishing it.

─────────

Father, thank You for turning my mountains into molehills. As I focus on Your name, I understand the power that comes with faith. In Jesus' name, amen.

ONE STEP AT A TIME

There was a man named Jabez who was more honorable than any of his brothers. His mother named him Jabez because his birth had been so painful. He was the one who prayed to the God of Israel, "Oh, that you would bless me and expand my territory! Please be with me in all that I do, and keep me from all trouble and pain!" And God granted him his request.

—1 CHRONICLES 4:9–10

The book *The Prayer of Jabez*—written about these two verses on a little-known Bible character—became a bestseller. I read numerous testimonies of people who prayed the blessing prayer, expecting their territories to be expanded. And I wondered why God did not tell us more about Jabez.

I thought, *Why not pray the prayer?* We had prayed others' prayers throughout the years, and it seemed to work, but I had a difficult time asking God to bless me. I had no problem praying for others with faith that they would receive healing or praying for those whose marriages needed a miracle. It was a different story when I began to pray for myself.

So I finally tried the book out. I read how Jabez's mother named him because he had been born out of pain. Jabez prayed that God would keep him from trouble and pain, that he would be blessed and his territory expanded. God granted his request. So today let's pray as Jabez prayed that our territory will be expanded, that blessings will come, that God will be with us in all we do and keep us from trouble and pain.

If you've ever wondered why your prayers were not answered or why you didn't have a sense of fulfillment, pray the simple prayer that God would use you. That you would be Jesus with skin on as you meet people in need every day. If Jabez could ask God to change his life and destination, you can too.

Take one step forward and watch God make a difference.

Father, I pray that You will use me, that I will be Jesus to those I meet, and that my territory will be expanded as You bless me so I can bless others. In Jesus' name, amen.

Day 89

TELL IT LIKE IT IS

Summing it all up, friends, I'd say you'll do best by filling your minds and meditating on things true, noble, reputable, authentic, compelling, gracious—the best, not the worst; the beautiful, not the ugly; things to praise, not things to curse. Put into practice what you learned from me, what you heard and saw and realized. Do that, and God, who makes everything work together, will work you into his most excellent harmonies.

—PHILIPPIANS 4:8–9 MSG

Paul wrote these words while facing some of the worst trials of his life. Despite the threats of pain and death while imprisoned, Paul had previously exhorted the Philippians not to worry but present their petitions to the Lord so that peace beyond understanding would guard their hearts and minds through Christ Jesus.

How could Paul, who was imprisoned in Rome for being a follower of Jesus Christ, instruct others to stay positive in everything?

Most of us probably understand the importance of praise, but praise doesn't always come easily when we're standing alone in a battle and we are uncertain of the outcome. We think of praise as being a result of victories.

In Christ we see joyful times, but what sets us apart as His followers is that we can remain steadfast in our beliefs through the most difficult trials. Jesus gives us strength not only to endure the most difficult times but also to grow through them. Despite trials and temptations, we can fill our minds with things that are worthy of praise.

Father, thank You for being God in the midst of trials and temptations. You gave me a promise to never forsake me, and You haven't. I shall always tell it like it is. In Jesus' name, amen.

Day 90

PAGE BREAKS

In peace I will lie down and sleep,
for you alone, O Lord, will keep me safe.
—Psalm 4:8

Have you ever wondered the purpose for page breaks? They are used to control where a page ends and another one begins. The negative spaces between paragraphs and chapters are places for the reader to digest what they just read, integrate it, and start fresh. It's just as important in life to determine the seasons of timeouts. It's so easy to be influenced by the demands of life, but then something catastrophic happens, which causes you to take a step back and determine what's truly important. That's your page break. Why does it often take something catastrophic to get our attention?

During the season when my dad was on his journey with dementia, my mom stepped back from a busy life of serving others to understand her journey for that particular season. After planting new churches, pastoring, and traveling throughout the world on missions, my mom knew she and my dad could no longer pastor their church as they had done for so many years. It was time for a "page break," so the decision was made that I would step up and become the senior pastor of our church.

I watched as my mother willingly cared for my dad and his care became her priority. She lovingly spent her days managing my dad's world until he began his transition to his forever home. As we stood around his bed, weeping as he drew his last breath, my mom whispered to him, "Serving you for fifty-two years was the greatest assignment of my life."

At this page break there would be no more content to the marriage that had begun for two young idealistic adults who wanted to reach the world for the kingdom of God. As I finish this book, I remember the night my dad passed. Before everyone left the house, my brother asked my mom what she needed. She told him she wanted the hospital bed removed from her room; tomorrow would be a new day.

Page breaks mean new beginnings.

———————

Father, as I take a page break during my seasons of difficulties, help me have the wisdom to understand what is important. Thank You for being my help. In Jesus' name, amen.

ACKNOWLEDGMENTS

As I ponder the reality that another book is being released that has come out of my spirit, I am so thankful to everyone who helped make my journey possible. There is no way this venture could have been accomplished without vital people in my life who take on the giant responsibility of accompanying me as I dream big and then see my dreams fulfilled. In fact, this book would not be in existence today without the most important people in my life that I call family.

As I watch my oldest son, Morgan, on the platform each Sunday singing and playing lead guitar in our Limitless band, and Lyncoln, my youngest, with numerous cameras always making sure that I am looking good in each stage of production, I am full of thanksgiving that God assisted me in becoming the mom that they so deserve. They were there when I was trying to find myself yet loved me despite me.

Of course, my mom is a vital part as we write our books. This woman knows how I think and process and allows that to flow through the pages of each new venture.

To my Real Talk Kim ministry staff, you are always working to carry out the vision given to me by God. You definitely order my world. I am amazed as I verbalize what I see, and you all seem to be hearing the same instructions from God. Watching you and our Limitless ministry staff work so effortlessly is truly amazing.

To the Real Talk Kim Inner Circle, All Access, and Masterminds, I am so thankful to God that He has given me the opportunity in this life to love and serve you. Let's keep accomplishing great things for the kingdom of God.

Of course, everything is pivotal on our Lord Jesus Christ. Without Your anointing and direction, nothing would have been accomplished. My life has been so totally changed because You did not give up on me.

ABOUT THE AUTHOR

Pastor Kimberly Jones, known as Real Talk Kim, is an entrepreneur, mentor, motivational speaker, entertainer, and bestselling author. Real Talk Kim has a successful weekly syndicated podcast and has appeared on *Preachers of Atlanta*, *The Dr. Oz Show*, *Chatter* talk show, BET, *Nightline*, and numerous podcasts, webinars, and radio programs. She is the senior pastor at Limitless Church in Fayetteville, Georgia. Kim is the proud mother of two sons, Morgan and Lyncoln.